AF481127

THE SHAMELESS LADY

MILLION WOMEN AT THE TOP!

Suvarna Hegde & Rajesh Bhat

ISBN
Paperback 979-8-89777-941-3
Hardcase 979-8-89906-259-9

Table of Contents

The Beginning... 2

To the 'Iron Lady Army' Members: A salute and a pledge!........... 3

1. An Oasis in the 'Desert' of 'Lost Hope'!......................7

2. A New Era?..21

3. The PAIN and the Need for 'A Movement'...................34

4. Wars in the Corporate: The Corporate 'Doormat'?............51

5. Wars in the Family: The 'Double Graduate Maid'.............77

6. The Battles of a Woman's Mind!...........................101

7. Shakti...123

8. The Tactics: Win Without Fighting 143

9. The C-Suite League 182

10. On a mission: The Iron Lady Army!.........................196

A new beginning...213

Acknowledgements...215

All the **stories** in this book are **REAL***!

These stories – of women who reached the **crore plus income**, the story of the **cancer survivor** reaching the **C-Suite**, the **CEO** who was **stuck,** and the story of abuse **by a father-in-law** – and the women behind them are an integral part of the movement!

The Beginning

"I felt like committing suicide.," said Maya, with her 'buddies' in the Iron Lady Army.

She continued, "I felt like I couldn't deal with **all the challenges**—whether at home or at work. Giving up seemed like the only option!

At that point, I was fortunate that a friend introduced me to Iron Lady. I could relate to the tactics that they were sharing. I could see the journey of thousands of women who had **already reached the top**.

I felt more confident as I implemented these tactics over the next few weeks. I started building on my strengths. I stepped into a new job, tackling every challenge at home and working with a newfound sense of confidence and control.

At first, many could not believe I had reached the **1-crore-plus income benchmark**!

It was a dream come true for me as well. I had not even believed I could speak up in these meetings! If I can do it, each of you is far more capable than I was!"

Maya's story above is a testament to the phenomenon power of the '**Shameless Ladies**' – who have decided to dream big.

They've **defied** the **odds**:
100+ women have reached **crore plus** yearly income!

They've reached **new heights**:
55+ women have become **CEOs!**

They've built exceptional **capabilities**:
In the last three years alone, thousands have earned over twice their previous incomes, and many have increased their incomes multi-fold.

They've dealt with the **toughest of challenges**:
A cancer survivor not only fought with cancer but also reached the **C-Suite!**

They've pushed boundaries:
Many came out of **toxic relationships** or environments to create a brighter future for their loved ones.

This book is a tribute to all these 'Shameless Ladies' – who have faced the toughest challenges – and are winning against the odds.

As part of this book, we will share many stories and tactics these women have used.

All the tactics are shared to move forward with our purpose:

Million women at the TOP!

Every story in this book is true, and we hope to create millions more stories of women.

We, the authors, have been privileged to experience firsthand the **enormous 'Shakti'** and exceptional capabilities of these fantastic women.

With the support of our cofounders and community members, this book represents our effort to elevate the movement to a new level.

This book is a WAR CRY, a shout-out to every woman:

That

YOU CAN.

You ARE

You WILL!

and

It is fine to be **shameless** about **your dreams** as well!

To the 'Iron Lady Army' Members

A salute and a pledge!

Dear Iron Lady,

You have trusted us, come together, and built the **Iron Lady Army**!

While we may be the official authors of this book, it is, in fact, the result of your efforts. These are your stories!

We, the founding team, take this opportunity to **salute your efforts** in following the tactics, navigating the challenges, and overcoming them.

Through this book and many other efforts, we also **pledge to increase our efforts manifold** – and take the movement to the next level, creating more ways to support every Iron Lady.

We seek your blessings as we undertake greater challenges!

- Suvarna Hegde
- Rajesh Bhat

Why a separate initiative and book for women?

We understand the enormous challenges that women face every day. These challenges have existed for centuries!

This book is an attempt to equip women with tactics and tools to deal with those.

We are not against men or consider men as enemies of women. Neither is our attempt to instigate anyone!

We believe in the immense 'Shakti' within women. Our work is all about enabling them to win using that 'Shakti'.

We have found that when women succeed, men around them tend to grow as well.

Chapter 1: An Oasis in the 'Desert' of 'Lost Hope'!

1. The Moment of Truth

Suvarna's Journey:

It was the 16th of April 2010. I was in tears. One moment, I was leading my team confidently.

The next moment, I was stunned and shattered.

I had overheard my male colleague, who held the same position and experience as me, casually discussing how he had negotiated and received a 'substantial increment' three months ago.

I realized that I was earning **40% less** than him.

Forty percent less!

I had poured my heart and soul into this project for over two years!

I had done way more than whatever my colleague had done.

The unfairness stung deeply. I'd worked tirelessly to deliver exceptional results, yet someone else reaped the benefits without putting in half the effort.

This wasn't the first time. I have experienced discrimination all my life.

I went to school in my village by walking 10 km each day. I have often been told that girls are not meant to study much or have goals.

The big gap!

Most of the girls in my village get married **around the age of 18**. Having studied in a Kannada-medium school, I had to fight numerous hurdles to pursue higher education.

None of the women in my family or the village left **their homes** to work outside the home.

I was the **first person** from my village to become **an engineer.**

          Chapter 1: An Oasis in the 'Desert' of 'Lost Hope'!

After becoming an engineer, I fought numerous battles to become a **team leader**. I was, by far, the **best team leader** in the department, as indicated by the feedback from my manager.

Yet, despite my top-tier performance all my life, men always seemed to get more pay, more opportunities, and more recognition.

I kept asking

"Why?"

2. The Truth for Every Woman!

I slowly realized I wasn't alone in this struggle. Most of my female colleagues and friends faced the same challenges.

<table>
<tr><td>

<u>Did you know:</u>
- Women hold only 12.7% of middle and senior management roles in India, as per LinkedIn and The Quantum Hub report.
- Women are interrupted 33% more in meetings, disrespected, and overlooked more often than men, as per a Harvard Business Review study.

</td></tr>
</table>

This was about more than money. It was about every dismissed idea, missed chance, and the subtle message that we 'were not enough.'

Why should we change ourselves to fit into a system built against us?

I reached out to mentors and asked them about the steps I could take to overcome these challenges. I began exploring ways to address the challenges.

Over the next three years, my career took off. I was able to reach three levels higher! My income went up by **four times**!

That's when I started thinking, why can't every woman implement the tactics that I used?

That's when I started sharing the idea of a movement with my other co-founders.

3. Rajesh's journey: Are you a man or not?

On February 23rd, 2025, we celebrated a milestone at Iron Lady Army: 100+ Iron Ladies joined **the crore-plus yearly income benchmark.**

The atmosphere was electric, filled with laughter, tears of joy, and stories of grit and determination.

As usual, **I was draped in a saree**, standing amidst a sea of accomplished women who had shattered glass ceilings and defied the odds to achieve their dreams.

As I looked around, I saw women who had overcome unimaginable struggles—women who had risen above societal constraints, financial challenges, and systemic bias.

Chapter 1: An Oasis in the 'Desert' of 'Lost Hope'!

They were proof that the right tactics and ambition could conquer even the harshest circumstances.

Celebration Event – Iron Ladies Reaching Crore-Plus Income!

I recalled moments when people questioned my choice to wear a saree.

I was asked, **"Are you mad? Why are you wearing a saree?"** At an airport, someone once asked, **"Are you a man?"**

These comments came pouring in **when I decided to wear a saree on a TEDx stage**.

Someone called it **'crazy,'** someone else called me **'namard' (not a man)!**

These moments, though challenging, provided me with a glimpse into the everyday scrutiny and judgment that women face throughout their lives.

Reflecting on the journey that led to the Iron Lady movement, I'm reminded of the journeys of some of the most extraordinary women in my life, starting with **my great-grandmother.**

　　　　Chapter 1: An Oasis in the 'Desert' of 'Lost Hope'!

My great-grandmother was **widowed at the age of 30 with five children** in a remote village in Karnataka.

She took on odd jobs to make ends meet.

When **I was 4 years old**, my most vivid memory of her was how **LOUD** she was.

Looking back later, I heard stories about how, as a **30-year-old, good-looking widow and single parent**, she was constantly hounded by society.

My mother, married at 17, had innumerable instances of abuse and torture. I witnessed many of these, even during my childhood, in the village where I was born.

Despite everything, she stood up for her children, my sister and me – and declared that we deserved a better life through education.

My sister and I were fortunate that our parents decided to move us out of the village in search of a better education, and they ensured that we both became engineers, the first in our village to do so.

Yet, even as time progressed and society evolved, bias persisted. We believed things might have improved when we were blessed with two daughters.

However, our daughters still faced stereotypical comments like,

"You're a girl, stick to being a girl,"

          Chapter 1: An Oasis in the 'Desert' of 'Lost Hope'!

They were told what games to play, their ambitions, and how far they could go. These stories are not unique; they are woven into the lives of countless women.

4. The beginning of a 'movement'

The first time Suvarna came up with the idea of creating a movement to empower women, we were unsure.

We began brainstorming with global leaders, including **Simon Newman, Sridhar Sambandam, and Chitra Talwar.**

They were kind enough to join us as co-founders and create the **Iron Lady movement**.

They brought their global experience of **leading billion-dollar businesses** and a purpose to make a difference.

The question that lingered in our mind was this:

> "Can we create a significantly better world for the next generation of women?"

Iron Lady has now grown into a movement with thousands of volunteers stepping in, providing a platform that enables every woman to dream big and achieve even more significantly.

Over 78,000 women have benefited from the movement and are rewriting the narratives and breaking barriers!

     Chapter 1: An Oasis in the 'Desert' of 'Lost Hope'!

5. Why War and not peace?

People ask us often, "Why are you speaking about war and winning for women? Should you not speak about peace?"

Women go through '**war-like**' situations and end up on the losing side often. That's why we still see such disparities in the world today.

Yet, society offers no real solutions, only expectations.

This book offers tactics that have worked for women to enable them to WIN – **without fighting** – so that peace is attained with a sense of accomplishment.

In the following chapters, we outline the kind of 'wars' that women experience and how they need to tackle those – through practical tactics.

<u>**Did you know:**</u>

In India, a **2019 McKinsey report revealed that 85% of women** face societal pressure to prioritize family over career, with many being told that ambition is **"unfeminine."**

These tactics have already worked brilliantly for thousands of women.

One such story below is of someone who won in all these wars to reach the top!

          Chapter 1: An Oasis in the 'Desert' of 'Lost Hope'!

6. How a Leader from a Big Four Firm Reached the Top.

Sixteen years!

That's how long Maya had given to the corporate world.

Sixteen years of late nights, early mornings, missed birthdays, and half-eaten dinners in front of a laptop screen.

Maya wasn't just tired—she was exhausted in a way that sleep couldn't fix.

She had a good title: **Director of a Big Four Consultancy**.

She put in the work, but the credit slipped through her fingers.

She saw men—less experienced and less qualified—rise while she remained stuck. She was expected to be a team player, to be patient, and to be grateful.

She suffered in silence in the room when she pitched an idea, only to hear a man repeat it five minutes later and get praised.

She was "too assertive" when she pushed back, yet **"not leadership material"** when she didn't.

And then there was home.

She was asked to focus more on her personal life:

     Chapter 1: An Oasis in the 'Desert' of 'Lost Hope'!

"Are you sure you should be traveling so much?" "Don't you think you can 'balance' a bit more?"

She carried it all. The invisible labor. The pressure to prove herself. The fear that maybe, just maybe, she wasn't good enough.

The final blow came quietly. It was another promotion, another missed opportunity, another moment when her contributions were acknowledged but not rewarded.

When she finally worked up the courage to ask why, her manager's response was polite but clear:

"We just haven't seen you at that level yet."

That was it. That was the moment.

"I felt **helpless and worthless**, despite being a director, and hence **resigned from the job**!" Maya mentioned.

For weeks, she sat with regret. The anger. The voice in her head whispered,

"What if they were right? What if this is all you were ever meant for?"

That's when she joined the Iron Lady Community.

At first, it was just a program. But then it became a mirror.

It forced her to remember what years of being sidelined had made her forget—her strength, value, and *right* to take up space.

     Chapter 1: An Oasis in the 'Desert' of 'Lost Hope'!

Maya stopped waiting for people to recognize her worth.

She negotiated and got a **40% salary hike** and expanded her territory and client base!

She learned how to navigate office politics without losing herself. She finally understood that she didn't need to work *harder*—she needed to work *more strategically*.

Over the next few months, she excelled in her job and advanced to a higher role in her next position.

She stopped apologizing for being ambitious. She mentored younger women and taught them to stand their ground, ask for more, and *own* their success.

Within **18 months, she moved into a new role: her income had grown by more than 250%**, and she now had a very exciting role as **Senior Vice President** in a global MNC!

She became the leader she once needed.

This is not just the story of one Maya.

This is the story of thousands of Iron Ladies.

They were often called '**Shameless**' for asking what they deserved.

However – they persisted, continued to dream, and stood for what they believed was theirs.

It's these 'Shameless Ladies' who have now built this movement!

                    Chapter 1: An Oasis in the 'Desert' of 'Lost Hope'!

7. An oasis in the desert of lost hope

An innumerable number of women fight the most brutal wars every day.

The challenges before us are significant.

We need a **movement, collective action** – not just small individual efforts!

Every woman's success chips away at the glass ceiling, creating pathways for others to follow.

Together, we can build a world where ambition is celebrated, equality is a norm, and every woman leads with courage and conviction.

As one participant beautifully expressed:

"**Iron Lady** is the oasis in the **desert** of **lost hope** for women."

8. Reflections

Growth begins for women when they question the 'realities' around them.

1. Have you ever wondered what your true net worth is? Have you ever considered what you 'should be earning' versus what you 'are actually earning'? What is the gap?

- The years of experience that I have:

- My ideal yearly income:

- My actual yearly income:

- The gap:

2. What opportunities have you missed so far in your career or life? What small actions can you take **starting from today**?

3. What would you like to accomplish by the end of reading this book? Can you reflect on how you can apply the tactics and stories from this book to inspire you to take your next steps?

The more you challenge the status quo, the closer you reach a world that you intend for yourself.

However, women who start thinking along these lines are often labeled 'Shameless'!

Time to reflect on one key question for yourself:

Are you willing to be **'Shameless'** for your dreams?

Chapter 2: A New Era?

"I was told I **was too emotional** when I **warned** them about the **challenges**. Two months later, **half of the people quit**, and the **project collapsed!**" shared a Senior HR Leader from the community.

1. The Era Long Gone: <u>Physical Power</u>

"His sword moved like lightning, and his strength matched that of a hundred warriors. He was a conqueror!"

For centuries, **power was held by those with brute strength**. Heroes were warriors and rulers who led armies, conquered lands and demonstrated physical might. Strength was the currency of leadership, and war was the ultimate battleground.

Societies worshipped kings and rulers for their military dominance. Women were excluded from leadership and deemed too **'weak'** to rule.

In this era, **mind and logic often took a backseat**, dismissed as secondary to muscle power.

But history doesn't stand still.

The moment guns became common, physical power lost its edge. The moment nuclear weapons took over, war was no longer about who had the most enormous army.

Just like that, brute strength became irrelevant.

2. The Current Era: <u>Mind, Logic, and Data</u>

"In God, we trust. Everyone else brings data!"

Once ruled by muscle, the world has now been overtaken by the **mind**. Today, **leaders are those who master data and logic**—not those who wield swords.

This transformation has propelled unprecedented advancements in technology, science, and efficiency. Algorithms dictate decisions, and data drives global strategies.

A world governed purely by logic can feel **cold, rigid, and dangerous**. Wars are fought through technology, not diplomacy. Humanity is often lost in numbers.

If this is the world we are building, what future are we leaving for our children?

3. The New Era: <u>Empathy, Intuition, Creativity and Energy</u>!

"Artificial Intelligence will never fully replace core human capabilities such as **empathy, leadership, collaboration, and creativity,"** Nandan Nilekani, Cofounder, Infosys.

Leadership is shifting. With AI handling data and automation replacing routine tasks, what truly sets great leaders apart is their ability to **connect, collaborate, and inspire**.

We're seeing this play out: Companies that prioritize empathy drive retention, innovation, and impact. Today's strongest leaders aren't the loudest or the most ruthless—they're the ones who listen, adapt, and build authentic relationships.

And who naturally excels at this?

WOMEN!

Yet, leadership still measures success in profits and policies, ignoring the people behind them.

We claim to lead with logic, yet inequality, crises, and wars persist.

Why?

Because leadership has dismissed the one thing that could create lasting change—human connection.

The future won't belong to those who are simply the smartest or the strongest. It will belong to those who can lead through the power of empathy.

4. The Strength of Empathy / Intuition / Energy!

"Why so emotional?"

"Calm down!"

Sounds familiar? You've heard it in boardrooms, at dinner tables, and even when you showed care.

Chapter 2: A New Era?

Our Era is here!

For centuries, qualities like empathy and compassion—the very things that make us human—have been dismissed as weaknesses. Society told us that strength means detachment and that leaders should leave emotions at the door.

But look at the world this mindset created.

History glorifies leaders who conquered through sheer force.

It's not just history—it's happening now:

                                  Chapter 2: A New Era?

- How often have you held back in a meeting; fearing being labelled "too emotional"?

- How often have you carried the emotional weight of your team or family without acknowledgment?

Society expects women to care without credit and lead without showing their hearts. But here's the truth:

Empathy is NOT a weakness—it IS **your superpower**—if respected and nurtured correctly.

It is what makes you connect, build, and create real change.

Research has proven that leadership that values empathy, innovation, and creativity is much more powerful.

Did you know:

Studies show that companies with more women in leadership outperform those without by 21% in profitability (Study by McKinsey, 2020).

Companies that realized this and have acted upon it are growing faster than others that don't!

Countries that realized this long ago – like Iceland, have created a new world order.

Increasingly, leaders, companies, and countries are recognizing this reality.

Chapter 2: A New Era?

There's no better time in humanity's history than now, when the need and collective realization of Leadership driven by empathy and women exist.

However, there's still a massive gap in intent and ground realities.

5. Empowering Visionary Leadership: Blending Heart, Intuition, and Energy

Despite unprecedented innovation, global challenges persist today.

Climate crises escalate, conflicts fracture communities, and inequality deepens. We have data, strategies, and resources, yet progress in many areas is slow.

Why? Because transformative leadership demands **more than logic**.

It requires **intuition** to sense unseen opportunities, **creativity** to reimagine solutions, and the **energy** to turn vision into impact—all anchored in empathy.

For women keen to shape the future, your time to LEAD is NOW!

a. When the Earth Burns, we need Leaders who Innovate with Courage!

During the COVID-19 crisis, countries **led by women** performed the **best**!

Chapter 2: A New Era?

Some leaders kept debating with logic and data!

Women in leadership know that authentic leadership thrives at the **intersection** of data, gut feeling, and empathy.

We must ask ourselves: Will you wait for perfect metrics or pioneer with courage?

b. When Wars Rage, Build Peace with Creative Resolve

Behind every conflict are women rebuilding homes from the rubble and mobilizing aid networks.

Leadership is not just about power—it is about **reimagining possibilities**.

Imagine a negotiator blending empathy with inventive diplomacy or a manager channelling team energy to bridge divides. For boardroom leaders, creativity means refusing to accept "how it's always been done."

Wars end when leaders dare to see **beyond the spreadsheet**—to the human stories demanding audacious solutions.

6. The Future <u>Needs</u> Leaders Who empathize, Innovate, Create, and Act

Organizations and communities that nurture the strengths of **Empathy, gut feeling, innovation, and creativity** – are thriving.
A world led by logic alone is a world of hollow victories.

Policies cannot hug a grieving mother, and data will not spark the next breakthrough.

The gaps we face—climate inertia, fractured communities, systemic inequity—are gaps in **data-centred leadership**.

To women redefining success:

Your intuition is your superpower. Your creativity is the catalyst. Your energy inspires movements. Lead with your mind and the grit and grace that turns empathy into impact. Trust yourself and nurture these much more!

Progress is not a spreadsheet—it is a legacy. Will you build it with both hands: one grounded in wisdom, the other daring to feel?

<u>Did you know:</u>

- Countries led by women have handled crises better, with lower death rates and stronger economies (Harvard Business Review).
- Teams with female leaders report higher engagement and innovation (Deloitte).

*The world needs **empathetic leaders**—women who will not only break glass ceilings but also **create a better future for us**!*

7. An 'emotional' Pushpa creates Mega Impact

Pushpa spent years **hiding in plain sight**. She was the 'co-founder and director.'

However, she was often called too emotional and too caring for the man's world!

She also carried a wound too deep to voice.

Her pain had no name, only weight—a weight that pressed against her chest **every time she stepped into a room full of men**. A childhood trauma she never spoke of, one that silently shaped her life, her confidence, and her choices. She built walls, avoiding confrontation, shying away from the spaces she had earned her **right to be in**.

For years, she convinced herself it didn't matter.

She had built a business – ground up – and was already successful!

She felt that maybe the **success could somehow erase the echoes of the past**. But silence is not the same as healing. And the more she tried to outrun her pain, the more it seeped into her present.

Sitting in a session at **Iron Lady**, she heard a phrase that shook her to the core:

"Your stories and 'crucibles' create your future!"

The words hit her like a flood. For forty years, she had locked away the trauma, believing that speaking about it

                              Chapter 2: A New Era?

would only invite judgment. But something shifted in that room, surrounded by women who carried their battles.

With a trembling voice, she spoke for the first time:

> "For 40 years, I carried this weight alone. I thought it was my burden to bear, my secret to keep.

> But I slowly realized that silence was never strength. Strength is facing it, owning it, and letting it go."

The moment was raw, but it was also freeing.

She realized her **exceptional empathy** was her unquestionable strength! The empathy came from her own **story and experiences**!

She began to **unlearn the hesitation, the fear, the ingrained belief that she had to be small to be safe**.

She strengthened empathy and much more from then on.

A new sense of Energy and Purpose!

She started using her voice in personal spaces and **boardrooms, meetings, and every interaction where she had once chosen silence**. She demanded to be heard, stood up for her ideas, and redefined what leading meant.

The transformation was unmistakable. She was no longer just **running an organization; she was leading it—FULLY, unapologetically**. The past no longer dictated her future.

   Chapter 2: A New Era?

And that's when everything changed.

Pushpa stopped waiting for permission. She **stepped into her power** and led her company, Garbhagudi, with unshakable confidence. She restructured the company, built a strong team, and positioned her brand as a leader in the industry.

She transformed how she introduced herself, worked with the other directors to redefine the company's identity, and together, created a business that was not only profitable but built to **create impact**.

But her success wasn't just in strategy but in the **story that she told the world**.

Pushpa introduced herself not just as a leader but as someone with a clear purpose.

She communicated that **purpose** powerfully to every team member. She inspired a sense of trust and empathy in each one!

She recreated the meaning of **Garbhagudi—a** divine place known for its **ethical values, and holistic approach to treatment**.

With the newly defined paradigm for the organization, GarbhaGudi became more than just a health centre—it became a beacon of hope.

That's how Pushpa, along with her co-founders, built a mega-organization that supports **thousands of families**.

                         Chapter 2: A New Era?

But more than that, she built herself!

"If you're labelled as 'emotional', you should know that **are powerful**! If you can lead with a sense of purpose and confidence, you can **change the world**!", Pushpa says.

8. The Shift from Data to Purpose

Leadership has evolved—from physical power to data-driven decisions.

But as AI takes over logic and automation, one thing remains irreplaceable: the ability to connect, understand, and **lead** with heart!

Write down the answers to these questions:

- What are the instances where you've been told you're too emotional? What was your response to that last time? How can you prepare for these instances next time?

- Based on Pushpa's story, what is your **intention** or purpose for your team and your loved ones? Write one situation or area wherein you will communicate your **purpose (with empathy)** powerfully.

   Chapter 2: A New Era?

In a world chasing efficiency, it is human empathy and intention that will define the leaders of tomorrow.

Women who dream of a better future for themselves and others are often called '**Shameless' and greedy**.

However, leaders who drive with a purpose– bring about changes for the better.

Are you ready to create a **new world** around you with a sense of **purpose** and **energy**, with the power of **empathy**?

Chapter 3: The PAIN and the Need for 'A Movement'

"I graduated from **IIM Ahmedabad 20 years ago**. I did tremendous work and built a good career. **Still, I lost my job recently due to politics and bias**," Anu, one of our participants, shared.

Why did she lose her job? Not because she lacked skills. Not because she was incompetent.

But because she could not navigate the unwritten rules of leadership and power.

This is not just her story. It is the reality of millions of women.

There are numerous initiatives and platforms, including those from corporations and governments, to support women.

Yet, we still have a long way to go regarding women reaching the TOP.

In the sections below, we explore some of the systems built to support women, why they fail, and what we need to enable women to win the toughest wars that they fight.

1. Schools and Colleges

Education should be a launchpad for ambition. However, for millions of young girls, it becomes the first roadblock.

The system is not broken in obvious ways; it is quietly failing them in the stories they read, the roles they are assigned, and the dreams they are taught to shrink.

A textbook shows a mother rolling out rotis in the kitchen, with the caption:

"Mom is in the kitchen making rotis."

On the next page, the father sits at a desk, deep in discussion with other men in suits:

"Dad is at a business meeting."

The message is clear. **One belongs at home. The other belongs to the 'world.'**

So, without realizing it, little girls shrink their dreams to fit the roles they have always seen.

They hesitate to say, "I want to be a scientist" because no one in their books, toys, or world looks like them in those roles.

Boys, meanwhile, grow up knowing they are expected to take charge.

It is no surprise, then, that when children picture a **CEO, a politician, or a business leader**—they picture a man.

The message girls get from this is: **This is NOT for you!**

So, when women enter the **workforce, they start with a considerable disadvantage**— before they even step into their **first job**!

                         Chapter 3: The PAIN and the Need for 'A Movement'

<u>Did you know:</u>

A **UNESCO study** revealed that Indian school textbooks often feature a significant imbalance, with male characters outnumbering females and women frequently depicted in traditional roles. At the same time, men are shown as leaders or professionals.

2. Diversity Initiatives

A community member of the Iron Lady Army secured a role at one of the **world's leading technology companies**. She was thrilled!

Her strategic communication, powerful pitching tactics, and relentless ambition had finally paid off!

But in her first week, reality shattered her excitement.

Her manager, in a casual conversation, dropped a statement that would stay with her for years:

"You are a **'diversity' candidate**! You only got this job because **you are a woman**. I wanted to hire 'my favorite **boy.**'"

It was not just a remark. It was a verdict that countless women in leadership roles hear in whispers, assumptions, and outright statements.

This is a reminder that no matter how skilled, accomplished, or deserving they are, their presence in the room is often questioned before they even get the chance to prove themselves.

Diversity initiatives are meant to create opportunities and level the playing field for women in industries that have historically sidelined them. But what happens after they walk through the door?

Instead of being valued for their capabilities, women who enter organizations through diversity programs often find themselves **immediately placed under suspicion**.

- Their ideas are **met with skepticism**.

- Their achievements are **credited to luck or lowered standards**.

- Their career progression **slows down, not because of lack of performance, but because of perceived 'handouts.'**

Even when they outperform expectations, they must prove themselves repeatedly—something their male counterparts rarely do. They do not just work to build their careers; they work to justify their existence in those careers.

The stigma is so deep that many women hesitate to apply.

Diversity hiring should recognize talent, not undermine it—until that shift happens, women will continue carrying the burden of proving their worth.

Women 'empowerment' programs

Many institutions and companies now offer **women-only** leadership programs.

      Chapter 3: The PAIN and the Need for 'A Movement'

The problem is that these programs focus on **soft skills and 'balance' aspects** —communication, emotional intelligence, and "balancing multiple roles."

They fail to train women in the winning tactics women need to grow in their careers.

3. Networking Initiatives

"Networking is the key to success."

Women hear it all the time. A few networking initiatives exist for women.

Do they help?

Superficial Conversations, Little Impact!

Too often, women's networking events become social gatherings rather than true career accelerators. Instead of being power hubs that open doors to leadership, they turn into:

- Chit-chat and coffee sessions with surface-level discussions that never translate into real opportunities.

- Motivational talks filled with feel-good advice but lacking actionable career-building strategies.

The problem is not that women do not network; these spaces often lack the structure and intent needed to drive real career impact.

4. Elite educational institutes like Harvard

"I was going through a program at **Harvard**. Unfortunately, I got some knowledge but could not apply that knowledge. **Hence, I quit**." mentioned Sirisha, who reached the **top position as Senior Director** using **Iron Lady Way**.

Some women work relentlessly to get into top-tier institutions—Harvard, IIMs, and world-renowned business schools—expecting these places to shape them into leaders. But even in these prestigious halls, something is missing.

a. Missing Tactics and Strategy for Women!

These institutions are exceptional in many ways.

However, when it comes to enabling women with real-world strategies for navigating power, office politics, and leadership battles.

Men in these leadership programs are trained to negotiate, influence, and expand their power.

Knowledge is NOT growth!

Women struggle to relate to those; they are given a different lesson plan: 'How to **balance**'!

The result? Women step into leadership environments believing competence is enough—when leadership is a game of power, positioning, and influence.

b. Representation in elite institutes

Even in the most elite leadership programs, women remain outnumbered. The numbers tell the truth:

- Women constitute only a tiny percentage of participants in leadership programs, even at top universities.

Diversity speeches will not fix this. Until universities actively develop more powerful and relevant curricula that are far more relevant to women, they will continue to fail the women they claim to empower.

5. Winning the Toughest Wars: Need for a Movement

When we studied the toughest wars that women fight, we realized that they fight the toughest 'wars' in these three areas every day.

a. The 'War' at Work

Women experience 'war-like' situations every day at work.

They get hired, promoted, and included in leadership at a **much slower rate** than men.

But it is not just about numbers. It is about **a toxic workplace culture that exhausts women with unrealistic expectations and office politics** that reward connections over competence.

b. The 'War' at Home

Even in 2025, women continue to bear the majority of household responsibilities—from managing the home to caring for family members. The expectation is that they will handle it all effortlessly while continuing to excel in their careers.

Meanwhile, many men focus solely on their jobs without the pressure of **"balancing it all."** Women, on the other hand, are often treated as if their careers are secondary.

c. The battles of a woman's Mind

Sometimes, the biggest battles are internal. Women hesitate to pursue leadership roles—not because they lack the skills, but because they have been conditioned to believe they need to be **"perfect"** before stepping up.

They second-guess. They shrink back. They worry about being seen as **"too ambitious"** or **"too much."** And while they hesitate, less qualified men take the opportunities.

d. Iron Lady Way: Win Without Fighting

Superficial solutions, motivational speeches, and basic certifications **do not enable** women to WIN the above **three most brutal wars.**

Women need platforms that enable them to '**Win Without Fighting**' the most brutal wars **in all the areas.**

Winning does NOT mean – **defeating** someone else or defeating men.

Winning is about accomplishing their goals and dreams with **good intentions** and **empathy**.

When women win, others around then also win – creating much more joyous families and winning teams.

Over the past eight years, we have developed a methodology through extensive research and collaboration with actual practitioners.

　　　　Chapter 3: The PAIN and the Need for 'A Movement'

We have piloted them, fine-tuned them based on feedback, and ensured they work!

The methods, templates, and tactics are collectively referred to as the **Iron Lady Way**.

The following chapters will explore some of these in detail: specific tactics for 'Winning Without Fighting'- the wars that are raging.

6. Building a ₹30 Crore Business from scratch in 3.5 years!

"Running a business is **not a woman's job**, especially in Kolkata." Minal was told.

Minal Bhagat is a well-known entrepreneur in Kolkata today.

But the journey to this point was far from easy. It was a path paved with battles that often left her exhausted, heartbroken, and questioning her worth.

When people meet Minal today, they see a confident, successful entrepreneur who built a ₹50-crore business from scratch. But they do not see the bruises she earned along the way.

Her career began in the unforgiving world of door-to-door sales. Many considered it a job beneath their qualifications, but Minal embraced it wholeheartedly.

          Chapter 3: The PAIN and the Need for 'A Movement'

"I remember walking through crowded streets, knocking on doors, and hearing 'no' after 'no,'" she once shared. "There were days when people slammed the door in my face before I could finish my sentence."

But the rejections were not the most challenging part. The hardest part was the isolation. As a woman in sales two decades ago, she was an anomaly. And people did not make it easy.

"There were **no proper toilets** for women. No safe spaces. I would attend meetings where men would smirk, as if wondering what a woman was doing there," she recalled. "I would sit alone during lunch breaks because I didn't belong to the 'boys' club.'"

The loneliness was suffocating. But Minal didn't let it break her.

The Tears That Taught Her Strength

One incident stands out vividly in her memory. She was in a high-stakes negotiation for a government contract, a deal she had worked on for over a year. The room was tense, and the man across the table was known for his aggressive tactics.

Halfway through the meeting, he slid a tissue box across the table and said, with a smirk:

"You might need this. **Women like you cry** when the pressure hits."

Minal froze. Her throat tightened. The sting of humiliation burned in her chest.

"I wanted to scream, to walk out, to cry. But then I heard this voice: 'You don't need their validation. Stay calm.'"

She pushed the tissue box aside, leaned forward, and said:

"I'm not here to cry. I am here to **close the deal.**"

That moment changed everything. She did not just secure the contract—**she won respect**. But later, when she got into her car, the tears she had held back streamed down her face.

"That day, I realized my tears were not a sign of weakness. They released the strength it took to hold my ground."

The Struggles at Home

Minal's battles were not confined to the office. At home, she grappled with the guilt of being an ambitious woman.

"There were nights when my son would ask me why I wasn't home for dinner, and my heart would break. I wondered if I was being a good mother," she said.

Society's judgment was relentless.

"Relatives would say, 'Why are you working so hard? Your husband earns well. Focus on your family.'"

The pressure to conform weighed her down. But deep within, Minal knew she was not built to live a life of 'just enough.' She wanted to create something meaningful for herself and for the generations of women who would come after her.

She tried various programs to overcome the challenges. However, her challenges were so intense – that she couldn't find solutions in any of those programs.

Chapter 3: The PAIN and the Need for 'A Movement'

She struggled to establish and scale her business.

The Iron Lady Transformation

In April 2019, she joined the Iron Lady Army and started practicing the **Iron Lady Way**.

She did not need sales lessons; she needed tools to manage her energy, emotions, and mindset and to enhance her capabilities in building and scaling her business.

"Iron Lady didn't just teach me tactics. It showed me how to stand tall when the world tries to push you down," she said.

The principle of *Playing Your A-game every Day became her anchor. She started applying it not just in high-stakes meetings but also at home.*

"I realized my family deserved my best self just as much as my clients did," she reflected.

She also mastered Shameless *Pitching Techniques.*

"For the longest time, I hesitated to ask for help. I thought it made me look weak. The Iron Lady taught me that asking for help isn't a weakness.

She began applying it everywhere—from requesting her family to share household responsibilities to negotiating better terms in business deals.

The results were transformative.

Minal secured a massive contract for over 1,600 classrooms in Odisha, a deal competitors had written off as impossible.

And she did it while maintaining her role as a present, loving mother.

The Breakthrough

Today, Minal's company has crossed ₹30 crore in revenue. But when you ask her about her most significant success, she does not mention numbers.

"My biggest success is when younger women in my team say, 'If Minal ma'am can do it, so can we,'" she says with pride.

She mentors other women through the Iron Lady community, teaching them to face corporate politics, self-doubt, and societal judgment with unyielding strength.

Minal's Message to Every Woman

When asked what advice she would give to women aspiring to break barriers, she did not hesitate:

"Do not shrink yourself to fit into someone else's idea of who you should be. Take up space. Speak with conviction. And never, ever apologize for wanting more."

And then, with a smile, she added:

"Tears are not your enemy. Let them flow when needed. But do not let them drown your dreams."

Minal Bhagat's story is not just her own. It is the story of every woman who has been underestimated, has felt the sting of doubt, and has dared to dream beyond societal expectations.

7. The Road Ahead

This book is not here to complain about wars; it is here to give you some of the tools to win without fighting.

Every chapter ahead is designed to arm you with specific, battle-tested strategies—the kind that no one has ever taught women outright.

This is not about small, incremental changes. This is about creating a force of women leaders who refuse to play by outdated rules.

The following chapters outline the method and ways of Winning those – and creating a much more joyful world.

8. Who is a Shameless Lady?

 She is the woman who refuses to shrink, apologize, or play by society's outdated rules about her dreams.

A **Shameless Lady** is not a rebel without a cause—she is a leader.

She dares to dream, rise, speak up, ask for more, and lead unapologetically.

In a world that thrives on women being polite, quiet, and self-sacrificing, being shameless is an act of power.

A Shameless Lady is empathetic; she utilizes her empathy to support and nurture others, enabling them to lead and succeed.

She is creating a better world for everyone!

9. Reflections

Reaching the next level in life or career often involves fighting various wars. Many give up after trying multiple options, but setbacks do not end the journey.

Write down:

1. What are my most significant work-related challenges?

2. What are my most significant challenges at home?

3. Where have I given up hope for growth, believing I will not be able to do it at all?

Begin the next chapter with a renewed mindset and focus on finding the solutions!

We will explore the various 'wars' in detail and how you can WIN those.

Women who speak the language of WINNING may be called **shameless or GREEDY**.

However, if you do not train yourself to WIN, you lose before you begin!

So, what is your next BOLD move towards 'winning'?

      Chapter 3: The PAIN and the Need for 'A Movement'

Chapter 4: Wars in the Corporate: The Corporate 'Doormat'?

Ramya did **exceptional** work for **12 months**. The project was a grand success. Excited about her growth, she went all prepared with all the work she had done during the appraisal cycle.

However, she was shocked when her boss told her,

'You need to be more visible!'

She was shocked. Her male colleague, who was **'more visible,'** got that promotion!

Her boss also mentioned casually,

'Anyway, **your husband is working**. You do not need so **much money or growth**'!

She had worked extremely hard throughout the entire year and produced all the results, while her colleague was more **'visible' and 'deserving.'**

1. Pre-historic Era

Her name was **Roop Kanwar**. She was just 18—vibrant, full of dreams, and newly married.

In January 1987, she left her family to join her husband, Maal Singh, in a small village in Rajasthan. Their union was brief—only eight months.

In September, tragedy struck. Maal Singh fell ill and passed away. They said Roop was grief-stricken. They said she was a dutiful wife.

But on **September 4, 1987,** something unimaginable happened. Roop was led to her husband's funeral pyre, draped in red, and surrounded by chanting villagers.

They called it a tradition.

Roop Kanwar was burned alive. Not symbolically. Not metaphorically. Flames consumed her young body as she sat atop her husband's pyre. She did not choose this. She was not asked.

They called it Sati.

This is from **1987! Not 1800!**

They called it sacred. But where was the sacredness in her screams? Where was the honor in watching a teenager's life reduced to ashes?

Another horror still exists in some villages—a **marketplace for wives** known as **Dhadicha Pratha**.

Women lined up like lifeless dolls, scrutinized for their ability to **"serve."** They are sold, not married.

These atrocities do not happen secretly. **They thrive in the open.**

From **Sati** to **Dhadicha**, these practices reflect a mindset that sees women not as humans but as possessions to be used, burned, or sold.

Women (and a few men) have had to fight these wars in society for centuries.

They continue to fight similar wars in **corporate boardrooms and offices** even today!

2. Similar Wars, new battlefields

In today's corporate world, patriarchy is alive, not in the fire of funeral pyres, but in the cold boardrooms where decisions are made.

Investors are more willing to fund a **man's business idea**, while a woman has to fight twice as hard to prove her worth.

Promotions, pay raises, and recognition still favor men, while women are expected to **"earn"** their place in spaces designed to exclude them.

Although the packaging has changed, the barriers remain disguised as performance metrics, cultural fit, or leadership style.

3. The Wars Women Face in the Workplace

Have you ever walked into a room and felt you had to prove you belonged there?

Ever spoken up in a meeting, only to be met with nods—until a man repeats the same point, and suddenly it is **"brilliant"?**

The Diversity Dilemma

Have you ever felt like whatever work you did it was still not **"enough"** to be taken seriously?

You are not alone.

Despite all our progress, the workplace is still not designed for women to thrive as it should be. Some of the biggest roadblocks women face are not always visible, but their impact is undeniable. And if we do not talk about them, we cannot break them down.

Let us discuss three significant challenges women still battle daily at work—and what needs to change.

4. Corporate Politics and Favoritism: The Unseen Hand That Replaces Women

"She's too aggressive."

"She's too soft."

"She's a mother now—her priorities have changed."

These are not just casual observations. These are **weapons**—used to sideline women, question their commitment, and disqualify them from power.

But beyond stereotypes, **intense office politics** plays an even dirtier game. Women are often the first to get played.

Why?
Because society still sees them as the weaker link.
Because most people assume she will not retaliate, she will not speak up and "adjust."

It is a lose-lose game,

Speak up, and you are **"too much."**

Stay quiet, and you are **"not leadership material."**

Make one mistake, and you are written off. Meanwhile, men with worse track records keep climbing.

You will see this happens all the time.

A woman works day and night to build a project from scratch—only to be replaced at the last minute by the boss's favorite **"sutta buddy."**

Why? Because he knows how to laugh at the right jokes, stroke egos, and play the game behind closed doors.

Or she returns from maternity leave, ready to pick up where she left off—only to find that she has been quietly pushed aside.

This is not bad luck. It is a **systemic sabotage**—dressed up as **"business decisions."**

Here is the most brutal part: **When politics turns ugly, women are the first to be thrown under the bus.**

So, let us stop pretending the playing field is level. It is not.

<u>Did you know:</u>

Mothers were **79% less likely to be hired** compared to non-mothers with identical resumes, according to a **study by Correll, Benard & Paik.**

Why This Happens

This happens because society has spent generations associating leadership, confidence, and ambition with men while expecting women to be nurturing, agreeable, and selfless.

These ingrained stereotypes create unconscious biases that influence decisions in hiring, promotions, and daily interactions—often without people realizing it.

An assertive woman may be seen as aggressive, while a man displaying the same trait is viewed as a strong leader. Women are also held to conflicting standards—they are expected to speak up but not too much and be ambitious but not unlikeable. These unspoken rules shape workplaces in ways that systematically hold women back, making it harder for them to be recognized, respected, and rewarded fairly.

Key Politics and favoritism challenges

Women in the workplace navigate a complex web of biases, stereotypes, and structural barriers that make it harder for them to advance in their careers. Understanding these barriers is the first step toward creating a fairer, more inclusive work environment.

Some of them:

- **Competence vs. Likeability Paradox**—Women who speak confidently or take charge are often perceived as aggressive or demanding, while men displaying the same traits are seen as strong leaders. This double standard forces women to balance being assertive and likable, making leadership roles harder to attain.

- **Motherhood Penalty** — Working mothers often face assumptions that they are less dedicated to their careers, leading to fewer promotions, missed opportunities, and lower pay. Meanwhile, fathers are typically viewed as more responsible and committed when they have children, reinforcing an unfair workplace bias.

- **Role Stereotyping** — Women are frequently steered toward supportive roles like HR, administration, or communications rather than leadership or technical positions. These biases limit their access to high-growth opportunities, concentrating key decision-making power in male-dominated fields.

Impact of These Challenges on Women

The barriers women face in the workplace slow their career growth, affect their confidence, financial growth, and overall well-being, and create an uneven playing field, making it harder for women to reach their full potential.

Let us break these down.

- **Slower Career Growth & Fewer Leadership Opportunities** – Women often struggle to climb the corporate ladder due to biases that question their competence or commitment. This results in fewer promotions, leadership roles, and opportunities for professional advancement.

- **Constant 'indirect attacks'** – Women go through an experience of 'being attacked' indirectly for no fault of theirs. They live in fear – not knowing where the next arrow will come from.

- **Increased Stress & Self-Doubt** – Constantly navigating workplace biases forces women to modify their behavior to fit unrealistic expectations, leading to stress, burnout, and a lack of confidence in their abilities.

How to WIN these corporate politics and battles!

Workplace biases and challenges are real. By recognizing these barriers and taking strategic action, women can break through glass ceilings, build confidence, and secure the opportunities they deserve.

Here is how to take charge and win.

- **Get out of the 'Sitting Duck' mode** — Be present to these and start developing your toolkit to deal with them. Too often, women become the 'sitting duck' in these situations—caught in the crossfires and finding it hard to deal with the challenges that come their way.

- **'Stand up' with a smile** — Be prepared to destroy people's biases. Flag biases and hidden glass ceilings and communicate about them. Bring attention to overall results. Do it proactively and ahead of time.

- **Keep yourself 'armed'** – Focus on what makes you unique and valuable. Recognize the skills and qualities that set you apart, and do not let biases make you doubt them. Keep yourself ready for various types of biases and challenges people throw at you!

5. Toxic Work Cultures That Drain Women's Ambition

"I came to work at 8 AM and stayed until 5 pm. I went back home and logged in again for an hour. He came to work at 12 pm and worked until 8:30 pm, **90 minutes less than me**. He was considered very hardworking, while I was seen as someone who **'leaves early,'**" mentioned Supriya.

Workplaces come with unwritten rules that put women at a disadvantage.

Cultures are defined – primarily by men – given that men hold top positions.

Diversity initiatives are ridiculed behind closed doors.

For women, this means constantly adapting to a system not built for them or risking being sidelined. These hidden barriers make equity a challenge, even when they go unnoticed.

Why This Happens

Many workplace traditions, from impromptu late-night meetings to networking over drinks, were shaped with a specific kind of worker in mind—men.

Women often navigate environments where leadership and advancement hinge on cultural norms that do not reflect their realities. The challenge is not just about proving competence; it is about overcoming structures that make participation more difficult than it should be.

Key Workplace Culture Challenges

Let us break down the hidden barriers that make it harder for women to rise.

- **Late-Night Work Culture as a Barrier to Advancement**—For some companies, staying late is still seen as a sign of performance. Even if women return and work at home, men are rewarded for 'extra hours.' Women are left wondering how they can show 'performance'!

- **Networking Over Drinks or smoke breaks: An Unfair Advantage** — Weekend drinks with colleagues might seem harmless, but they are where actual career moves happen in many workplaces. Most women do not prefer networking over drinks or smoke breaks. Women lose out—not because they lack talent, but because they were not in the right room at the right time.

- **Leadership Roles: 'Strong,' Male-Dominated Space** — Many companies, even today, hesitate to see women as leaders. Fifteen years ago, it was rare to find a woman in a CEO or CFO role, and while progress has been made, old mindsets have not entirely shifted.

The Harsh Impact of Cultural Roadblocks on Women

Workplaces claim to champion diversity, yet women still face invisible barriers that hold them back. From missed opportunities to the constant need to prove themselves, the struggle is real—and exhausting.

Let us break down how these cultural roadblocks impact women every day.

- **Opportunities That Stay Out of Reach** — Women work as hard as their peers, yet leadership roles and high-impact projects often pass them by. Despite their talent, they remain stuck while others move ahead, not because they lack ability but because the system favors a different mold.

- **Constantly Having to Prove Their Worth** — Women are expected to 'prove' that they have done the work – since there are environments where 'out of sight' means 'out of mind' and 'non-performance'!

- **Moving out, Not by Choice, But by Necessity** — When every step forward feels like a battle and recognition never comes, many women decide to walk away. They are tired of fighting a system that refuses to see them, not because they lack drive.

How to WIN in these challenging cultures

You do not have to play by these outdated rules to WIN!

Here is how to take charge and navigate these cultural roadblocks like a strategic leader.

- **Overcommunicate:** Keep your focus on the 'big picture' of business and develop a habit of overcommunicating about results, work, and targets. Make it a habit to always show 'your worth'! Get out of the habit of thinking, **"They will understand."**

- **Call out the cultural roadblocks with a smile:** Without indulging in unnecessary arguments, start calling out the cultural biases. Do this with some humor or sarcasm if needed!

- **Build allies in various teams —** Ensure enough people from multiple teams are 'on your side.' Find ways to engage with them humbly while providing and supporting them through win-win conversations.

6. Lack of Networks and Mentors Holding Women Back

"I don't go **out for drinks**. I had seen many **men bond over a smoke or a drink**, and I used to think I could only find **mentors over a drink**," mentioned Roshni in one of the community sessions.

Finding the proper support is an uphill task for women. Mentors and sponsors open doors, offer guidance and advocate for career growth. Yet, women often find themselves navigating their careers alone.

Men, on the other hand, benefit from informal and formal mentors

They gain mentors who guide them and sponsors who push them forward. For women, these connections are not as accessible, making leadership roles feel out of reach.

<u>Did you know:</u>

Women are significantly less likely than men to receive their first promotion to a managerial role—a gap that has shown slight improvement, according to Women in the Workplace 2024 by McKinsey & Company.

Why This Happens

Men often find mentors who see a younger version of themselves, making career advice and leadership opportunities a natural part of their growth.

Women find it hard to network in these spaces, given that they experience a sense of exclusivity to them.

They are left navigating their careers alone, working twice as hard to be noticed for leadership roles that seem effortlessly within reach for their male peers.

Even structured **mentorships,** if they exist at all, fail. People tend to treat them **as formalities** rather than being able to build deeper connections and create impact.

Many times, women find it difficult to share their **fundamental limitations and challenges** with colleagues – with the fear of being exposed to **more attacks**!

Lack of Networks and mentors holding women back

The lack of strong mentorship and sponsorship is not just an inconvenience—it creates real barriers to women's career progression:

- **Missed Opportunities for Growth** – Without sponsors advocating for them, women are often overlooked for high-profile projects and leadership roles that accelerate career advancement. Their male peers, with more vigorous advocacy, move ahead faster.

- **Pay and Promotion Disparities** – Men are often promoted based on potential and sponsors, while women must repeatedly prove their worth. Without sponsors challenging this bias, women remain stuck at lower levels for years.

- **Developing wrong capabilities or choosing wrong career paths**—Women find it very hard to understand what capabilities they need to build, what career paths exist, and how to make those. They take 'certificate courses' or develop 'junior-level' capabilities, which do not help them grow further.

How to Take Charge and WIN

Breaking through these barriers is not easy, but it is possible. Here is how you can take control of your career and secure the mentorship and sponsorship you deserve:

- **Purpose-based networks— Join professional groups where women uplift women and** understand and develop 'purpose' based conversations. Do not wait for the right mentor or network to find you—put yourself in spaces where growth happens.

- **Find WIN-WIN opportunities**—Sponsorship is not just about asking for help—it is about showing value. Identify senior leaders in your organization and take the initiative on strategic projects that align with company goals. Build formal win-win connections with people 2-3 levels above you and engage with them continuously over time.

- **Find specific gains with mentors with different strengths outside your workplace** — Instead of mentors who will solve ALL your problems, identify various types of mentors and look for specific answers. Some mentors who are complementary – someone who shows you how to manage your weaknesses. Finding mentors outside of your workplace is key.

7. Stuck? It is Time to Shift Gears

Imagine a world where every woman dreams and navigates corporate and societal challenges thoughtfully!

Where workplaces are brimming with powerful women at the TOP.

What would it take to create such a world? The answer lies in a collective shift—a cultural transformation where ambition is celebrated, not questioned.

The question is: What is stopping us?

8. Top Pitfalls

What common pitfalls can trip women up in the workplace, and what do some high-achieving women do to rise above them?

Here are a few reflections to help you take charge of your career journey.

Even the most ambitious women can unknowingly fall into these traps. They are often so ingrained in our everyday thinking that we do not even realize they are there—until we start noticing missed opportunities like promotions, pay raises, or leadership roles slipping through our fingers.

- **"They'll just understand."**

It is easy to think that hard work alone will get you noticed. After all, you are putting in the effort. But here is the thing: workplaces do not always recognize silent dedication. To stand out, you must make your achievements visible. Speak up about your wins and advocate for yourself.

- **Waiting for the 'Right Time'**

There is always a reason to wait, isn't there? More experience, a more significant project, a better moment. But here is a secret: men often negotiate first and grow into the role later. The 'right time' is when you decide it is time. Do not let fear of not being ready hold you back.

- **'My work will speak for itself'**

Women believe that their work should speak for itself. They end up thinking that given the amount of work I've done, they

    Chapter 4: Wars in the Corporate: The Corporate 'Doormat'?

should notice and be fair. Your hard work can go unnoticed without visibility, building your profile, and strategic positioning. Ensure you are seen as a leader, not just someone who does the work behind the scenes.

- **Avoiding Conflict to Keep Peace**

Many women hold back from pushing back in meetings, afraid of being labelled 'bossy' or 'difficult.' But here is the truth: leadership often involves stepping into discomfort. Power is not handed to you—it is something you claim. Do not be afraid to challenge the status quo when it matters.

- **Not Setting Boundaries and Saying 'Yes' Too Often**

It is easy to say yes to everything, thinking it will help you get ahead. However, taking on extra tasks that do not align with your goals can drain your time and energy. Remember: your focus should be on what helps you grow as a leader. It is okay to say no when something does not move you closer to your aspirations.

9. Iron Lady Way: How Women Are Winning

Thousands of women are winning corporate battles daily using the **Iron Lady Way**.

Below are some of the most critical steps they are taking.

- **'Pitch' Ahead of Time – using 'Shameless Pitching' tactics.**

They do not wait for annual performance reviews to plead their case. Instead, they initiate conversations early, armed with strategies, a track record of impact, and a clear ask.

They are building themselves up using the tactics called 'Shameless Pitching' (details in chapter 8).

- **Speak Up – using The Unpredictable Game**

They do not let self-doubt or social conditioning hold them back. They speak with authority, make their ideas heard, and push back when interrupted. If someone attempts to overshadow their voice, they reclaim their time with a simple but firm: "I wasn't finished yet." They practice and play The Unpredictable Game (details in chapter 8) to win.

- **Build Strategic Alliances – Because Influence Opens Doors**

They know that career success is not just about what you do but about who speaks for you when you are not in the room. They cultivate sponsors, not just mentors. These women are intentional about networking—not for socializing, but for strategic career moves.

- **Claim Credit without Apology – No More Playing Small**

They do not downplay their contributions or credit "the team" when they lead the initiative. They own their wins and ensure their achievements are recognized at the highest levels. They understand that visibility matters—because if leadership does not see their impact, they will never be considered for the next big opportunity.

- **Invest in Their Leadership Brand – nurturing the Shakti!**

They do not rely on their work to speak for themselves; they actively build their Differentiated leadership brand. They position themselves as experts by nurturing their Shakti (details in Chapter 7). They leverage every platform available to showcase their insights, making them impossible to ignore.

These women are not waiting for change—they are creating it. So can you!

Below is the story of Sharmistha, who used these techniques to achieve mega breakthroughs!

10.   Sharmistha's Leap: ₹1 Cr Income & 2-Level Jump—While 6 Months Pregnant

The Crossroads of Uncertainty

Despite her expertise in data analytics, **Sharmistha faced biases and glass ceilings.** While she excelled at her job, her bosses considered her **too weak, soft-spoken, and introverted.**

In meetings, her ideas were often **ignored by senior colleagues.**

When she applied for jobs, one interviewer remarked,

> **"You are qualified but lack 'executive presence.'"**

—a coded critique she recognized as gendered bias. Frustrated, she turned to her mentor at the Iron Lady Program.

She asked,

"How do I combat the perception that women belong in support roles, not leadership?"

Becoming Indispensable: Leadership Brand

Determined to **change the narrative,** Sharmistha spent weeks refining her communication. She began presenting her ideas with power and assertiveness, adopting a more substantial presence.

At first, she hesitated, never having spoken in public forums. But as her confidence grew, she started **sharing insights on professional platforms.**

She positioned herself as a **strategic thought leader,** publishing articles and engaging in industry discussions.

Her breakthrough came when she authored a whitepaper, How Silent Data Swung the Mandate, analyzing voter trends in **India's 2019 elections.**

Pregnancy and Prejudice

As Sharmistha gained **visibility** and was on the **brink of a promotion,** she discovered she was **pregnant.** Undeterred, she continued building her **leadership brand.**

Six months into her pregnancy, she was interviewed for a role two levels above her current position.

She prepared rigorously—crafting business roadmaps, honing negotiation skills, and seeking guidance from mentors.

After five intense interview rounds, **she secured the job—** negotiating a maternity break, even though company policy did not allow one so soon after joining.

Maternity Leave as a Leadership Test!

During her leave, Sharmistha stayed visible. Her mentors pushed her: **"Use this time to build authority. Stay relevant."**

She continued sharing insights, maintaining strategic discussions with her bosses, and keeping herself engaged in key projects.

Even on break, she contributed strategic ideas, ensuring she remained indispensable.

Promotion after 8 months of Maternity

Returning to work, Sharmistha encountered cultural resistance. A client requested a male lead, citing **"concerns about emotional decisiveness."** She took charge of the project herself, delivering a 30% efficiency gain.

When a senior leader questioned her ambitious strategy, she responded, **"Ambition is the baseline. Let us discuss why it's seen as a flaw."** By year's end, her team's revenue contribution had **surged by 45%.** Her relentless focus on **scalable solutions** earned her a **promotion.**

Yet, bias lingered—executives slashed funding for her AI initiative, dismissing it as **"too experimental for a woman-led team."**

Sharmistha continued to push harder and keep positioning herself, earning a promotion within 8 months of returning from the break.

End of Year 2: Executive VP & Crore-Plus salary

By 2023, Sharmistha's leadership brand had redefined her trajectory. She navigated challenges, built influence, and **negotiated a ₹1 crore+ annual package**—a 400% increase in two years!

She said at an industry forum, **"I do not 'lean in. I reconstructed the table!"**

"My brand is not luck," she tells cohorts. "The tactics I used were the weapons built through mentorship. Grab attention. Be known!"

Redefining the Ceiling

Today, Sharmistha's LinkedIn bio reads: **"Executive VP | 40 under 40 Data Leader"**.

Her journey—from overlooked professional to crore-earning executive—proves that barriers are dismantled through resolve and mentorship.

She says,

"Grand gestures don't shatter glass ceilings,"

"They crack daily, one audacious decision at a time."

11. The 'Shameless' Lady: When Speaking Up Becomes a Problem

"She's so shameless."

You have heard it. Maybe whispered in hallways. Sometimes, it is said out loud, like a warning!

A woman who negotiates her salary? Shameless. A woman who questions her manager? Shameless. A woman who does not apologize for ambition? Shameless.

This label is not just a word. It is a weapon.

In most workplaces, the moment a woman decides she will not *adjust* anymore, the moment she starts *demanding* what is rightfully hers—she is no longer the "good girl." She becomes "too much." And suddenly, she is carrying a new tag: **shameless**.

But let us call it strategic courage, the courage that makes people uncomfortable because it disrupts norms.

The 'shameless' tag is society's way of policing women into silence. Into obedience. Into invisibility.

But here is the truth no one says aloud:

- Men interrupt in meetings = confident.
- Women do it = shameless.

- Men negotiate = assertive.
- Women negotiate = shameless.

- Men promote themselves = ambitious.
- Women promote themselves = shameless.

If reclaiming your time, voice, and ambitions makes you shameless—**own it**. Let them be uncomfortable.

Because every powerful woman was once called shameless—before she was named a **leader**.

12. Reflect for a Moment

You have just confronted some uncomfortable truths about how society treats ambitious women—from subtle judgments in corporate boardrooms to horrifying cultural traditions.

Now, pause and write down:

1. What are societal or workplace biases that I have accepted so far, based on whatever I have read in this chapter?

2. What is the impact of these biases on my life so far?

3. What are one or two steps I can take to deal with societal or workplace challenges?

It is time we reflected as leaders:

What can we do to create **workplaces** where **women thrive**?

Chapter 5: Wars in the Family: The 'Double Graduate Maid'

"I'm a **double graduate**. I was highly **successful at work**. However, I felt forced to **sacrifice my career** and live like **a maid** at home!" **Jyoti's voice shook,** not with anger but with sheer exhaustion.

We've heard this story too many times. Women who are brilliant, capable, and full of ambition are trapped in a world that takes them for granted.

At home, they're expected to 'serve'!

<u>Did you know:</u>
Women spend, on average, 3.2 times more time than men on unpaid care work—4 hours and 25 minutes per day compared to 1 hour and 23 minutes for men, according to Care Work and Care Jobs for the Future of Decent Work by the International Labor Organization.

The heartbreak?

When they voice those dreams, they're met with raised eyebrows, disapproving glances, and condescending words:

"Why do you need more? Isn't this enough?"

But is it? Is it enough to give everything and receive so little in return?

What if we built a world where their dreams weren't just tolerated but nurtured?

A world where they were not just supporters of success but the ones leading the way?

Is this just a fantasy?

Can it be real?

Thousands **of women** are already stepping up, reclaiming their voices, and rewriting their stories.

They learned that ambition is not selfish, leadership isn't reserved for a few, and they are just as worthy of success as anyone else.

If you have ever felt unseen, unheard, or underestimated, this is your call to rise.

Your dreams matter. Your ambitions are valid. Your story is not over.

1. The 'Wars' That Women Fight in The Family!

No matter where she is in the world, every woman carries a weight that often goes unseen. A weight is placed on her shoulders by family expectations, societal norms, and cultural traditions that dictate who she should be, how she should live, and what she should prioritize.

CEO at the workplace.
Maid at home?

The CEO; treated as a maid?

From career sacrifices after marriage to the never-ending burden of unpaid labor at home, women are constantly expected to give, do, and be more—without ever asking for anything in return.

Worst of all? They are pushed to believe this is their choice.

When women try to break free from these expectations, they are met with guilt, judgment, and resistance.

These are not just individual problems—they are global issues that prevent women from living on their own terms.

      Chapter 5: Wars in the Family: The 'Double Graduate Maid'

Let us break them down.

2. Marriage: The Burden of Being a 'Good Wife'!

Marriage is supposed to be an institution of joy and togetherness. However, marriage becomes one of the biggest hurdles to growth for many women.

"Women belong in the kitchen!"

"You should be like Sati Savitri!"

These kinds of sentence words still break the dreams of many women today.

Marriage is often seen as a new beginning, but for many women, it becomes the end of the life they dreamed of. Across the world, talented and hardworking women leave their jobs—not because they want to, but because they got **married.**

Family pressure, in-laws' demands, and society's rules slowly push them away from their careers, making them choose between being a **"good wife"** and following their **dreams**.

<u>Did you know:</u>

In 2024, gender inequality persists in India's workforce. **A World Bank report shows that 13% of employed women quit after marriage** (Times of India).

Instead of growing in their careers, they are given household duties. Instead of being seen as capable professionals, they are told their husband's success matters more. Their dreams do not disappear, and they are forced to give up. But should marriage mean the end of a woman's ambition?

Why Does This Happen?

- **Deep-rooted societal beliefs and family expectations:** Many cultures still see a woman's primary duty as managing the home, not building a career. In-laws and husbands often expect her to prioritize household responsibilities over professional growth.

- **The 'good wife' stereotype**: Women are praised for sacrificing their ambitions for their husbands' success. Those who choose to work are often made to feel guilty for not being "good wives" or "good mothers."

- **'Insecure' or non-supportive husband**: Many women do not have encouraging partners or families, making it harder to balance career and marriage. We have often encountered insecure or jealous partners or family members who've derailed the careers of women.

These pressures force countless women to give up their careers—not because they want to, but because they feel they have no choice. But is that the only way forward?

Win the Wars at home without fighting!

     Chapter 5: Wars in the Family: The 'Double Graduate Maid'

Winning the battle at home is not about fighting with everyone!

Winning this battle means you choose to commit to your dream as much as to your family's needs.

But if she believes she deserves both, she will find a way. Confidence is the first step to reclaiming her future.

- **Master the Principle of 'Maximize':** Commit to **'AND.'** Women who have grown up in the community have constantly practiced the language of a great career AND a happy personal life. Not for we call this the principle of 'Maximize.'

- **Negotiate WIN-WIN at home:** Create and move towards situations of WIN-WINs – at home. Communicate your dreams and aspirations with passion and intent.

- **Find Resources That Support Your Growth:** Whether you need a good maid, a driver, or other different ways of getting things done, you must find more resources to manage things.

- **Stand Up for Yourself often:** Leadership begins at home. Own your ambition, voice your needs, and do not hesitate to speak up for your space, time, and priorities.

Marriage should not be a full stop to your ambitions. It should be a new chapter where you thrive personally and professionally.

Case Study: A Good Wife Shouldn't Focus on Her Career!

"I used to be a marketing manager, then I married."

Pooja said, her voice steady but laced with something unspoken!

She was not looking for sympathy. She wanted to understand why her ambitions became negotiable when she became a **wife**.

Before marriage, she thrived in her job, brainstorming campaigns, leading projects, and making an impact. But when her company downsized and she was let go, no one saw it as a setback; it was inevitable.

"Maybe it's for the best; now you can focus on your REAL responsibilities."

Her mother-in-law had said.

At first, she thought she would get back to work soon. But months turned into years. Every time she brought it up, she heard the same responses—

"Your husband earns well; why do you need to work?"

"Who's going to take care of the house?"

One evening, her father-in-law casually remarked,

"Girls these days are so ambitious. But family should come first."

He meant it as an observation, not an insult. But something about the way he said girls these days stung. As if ambition was a phase. As if her dreams were something to outgrow.

She said nothing. Just walked away.

She tried applying anyway. But rejection emails came faster than interview calls. Recruiters barely considered her after seeing the gap in her résumé.

The few interviews she got left her feeling out of touch—she struggled to explain why she had been away for so long.

She started thinking.

"It is difficult to start again after such a long gap."

Some days, she questioned if it was worth the effort. Maybe everyone was right; perhaps she should just let it go.

But she refused to accept that.

When she joined Iron Lady, where she realized she was not alone—many women faced the same struggle.

Slowly, she rebuilt her confidence. She started upskilling, attending webinars, and networking with old colleagues.

The next time she interviewed, she did not just explain her gap—she talked about the skills she had worked on during that time.

It still was not easy. She faced **weeks of setbacks**. But this time, she kept going.

Eventually, she built enough confidence and landed a good job with a 25% hike.

When she told her husband, his first question was,

"Will you be able to manage everything?"

Pooja's answer was clear.

"I'm sure you're there to support as well!"

She was not asking for permission. She had decided!

Women generally don't choose to give up their careers. They are made to believe they should.

Pooja chose differently.

3. The Impossible Standards of Motherhood

"A good mother always puts her child first."

This phrase is repeated so often that it feels like the ultimate truth.

Society expects a woman to give up everything—her career, her passions, and sometimes even her identity—for the sake of her child.

If she dares to want more? She is judged, ashamed, and made to feel guilty.

Motherhood is not just about raising a child but also about meeting impossible expectations. A mother who stays at home is told she is not contributing enough, and a mother who works is told she is not 'present enough.' No matter what she does, it is **never enough**.

But is this what motherhood should be?

Why Does This Happen?

Unrealistic societal expectations – Mothers are often expected to prioritize their children above all else, frequently at the expense of their personal dreams and career aspirations.

Guilt and judgment – Working mothers are often pushed into guilt for not being available 24/7, while stay-at-home mothers are frequently judged for not contributing financially. Regardless of the choice they make, they will face criticism.

The idea that a good mother sacrifices'—Women believe that being a good mother means putting themselves last. Their ambitions, health, and personal growth are seen as less important than their role as caregivers.

These pressures force countless women to give up their dreams—not because they want to, but because they feel they have no choice. But does it have to be this way?

Win the Battle of 'Motherhood'

The real challenge is societal expectations and the internalized guilt that so many mothers carry. A woman who believes she must choose between being a good mother and having a fulfilling life will always feel torn.

A mother who understands that **she deserves both** can redefine motherhood.

- **Break the Sacrifice Myth:** Being a good mother is not about giving up who you are. It is about showing your child how to live with courage and purpose.

- **Protect Your Ambitions:** You deserve a fulfilling life — and your child deserves to see what that looks like. A thriving mother raises thriving children.

- **Lead by Example, Not by Perfection:** Forget the myth of doing it all. What matters is showing up with strength, clarity, and direction. That is what your child learns from.

- **Choose Legacy Over Guilt:** There is sufficient research to demonstrate that children of working mothers tend to grow up more independent and successful. Do not chase perfection — model purpose.

Case Study: A mother who grew four times in 2 years.

"Should I continue working? I do not want to quit – however, the pressure is too much!"

Riya asked in a workshop.

     Chapter 5: Wars in the Family: The 'Double Graduate Maid'

Her parents asked her to quit her job, but she loved working. Her husband asked her to decide soon.

Her career was growing at a breakneck pace, and she thoroughly enjoyed her work.

However, after her second child, everyone in her family believed she should quit.

Her mornings started in chaos—half-eaten breakfasts, last-minute school prep, and urgent work emails buzzing on her phone.

At the office, she was struggling to focus.

By the time she got home, exhaustion had hit like a brick.

Riya tried harder. She stretched her limits, worked late, woke up earlier, skipped meals, and reduced her breaks. And yet—

Her family kept saying,

"You're not there for your child."

And the worst voice of all? Her own.

She felt as if she was failing—at everything. She hated herself for it.

During her Iron Lady workshops, she got suggestions about **COMMITTING to a path** and negotiating with everyone to deliver on that path.

She decided to manage these powerfully while also ensuring her career grew.

She negotiated far more with her family and at the workplace.

She put in enormous effort to hire another maid she could rely on.

At work, she stopped apologizing for being a mother. Instead of hiding her struggles, she negotiated:

"I want to take on a high-impact project! I will deliver results and expect to be promoted if I perform."

She demonstrated her worth much more at her workplace.

At home, she stopped trying to be everything and started **leading.**

Within 2 years of her second child's birth, she moved up by two positions in her office.

She moved into another company with a better hike!

She was **earning four times more** compared to what she was earning in just 2 years!

And her child? Thriving—growing up, watching a mother who never gave up, learning what real strength looks like. Her older son had started doing better in his studies, became more confident, and once told her,

"Mumma, when I grow up, I want to be like you."

This is not just Riya's story. This is the story of **thousands of mothers** who have mastered the **Iron Lady Way**!

        Chapter 5: Wars in the Family: The 'Double Graduate Maid'

4. Being the perfect daughter and daughter-in-law

"My father-in-law was trying to abuse me sexually. I had no clue how to handle it – I was worried that I would be blamed."

We have heard about the above situation many times in the community.

When women get married, they are often told, "Treat your in-laws as your parents. You do not belong to 'this family' from now onwards anymore."

She is told,

"Make sure your in-laws are always happy!"

With the commitment to make their in-laws happy, many women spend their lifetimes sacrificing all their dreams.

This expectation is deeply ingrained in many cultures, particularly in India, where women are often seen as the glue that holds families together.

But this really means that a woman's career, dreams, and even personal choices must be subordinate to family expectations.

If she dares to set boundaries or pursue her ambitions? She is seen as selfish, rebellious, or not **"family-oriented"** enough.

For many women, this pressure is suffocating. They are expected to seamlessly balance their careers, homes, and relationships without complaints, breaks, or personal desires. But is this what being a good daughter or daughter-in-law means?

Why Does This Happen?

The Pressure to Always Be Available

- Daughters-in-law are often expected to prioritize family over career, regardless of their professional success.

- Even working women are expected to handle household responsibilities without support.

The Burden of Tradition vs. Aspirations

- Women are caught between aspirations and deeply rooted traditional expectations.

- Breaking away from traditional gender roles often leads to criticism from family and society.

Emotional Manipulation

- Women who set boundaries or make independent choices are made to feel guilty for **"not caring enough."**

- The idea that a woman's primary role is to serve the family discourages personal ambition.

We don't want to depend on 'her'!

- Many women struggle to convince their families that their careers are as important as their male counterparts.

- If they seek career advancement, they are often told that their work is just an addition or distraction. You are expected to manage everything at home without compromise anyway.

These expectations force countless women to compromise their dreams—not because they want to, but because they feel they have no choice. But does it have to be this way?

Winning vs 'Being Perfect.'

The real challenge isn't just societal pressure but the deep-seated belief that self-sacrifice is the only way to be a good daughter or daughter-in-law. A woman who believes she must constantly prove herself to her family will always feel a sense of inadequacy.

A woman who understands that she has the right to pursue her ambitions can redefine what it truly means to be a daughter or daughter-in-law.

- **Redefine What It Means to Be 'Good':** Being a good daughter-in-law is not about erasing who you are. It is about living your values while honoring the ones you share with your family.

- **Build an Equal Partnership at Home:** Involve your husband as your growth partner who champions your ambitions and helps shape a family that thrives on equality.

- **Lead Without Apology:** State your boundaries, speak your truth, and stop overexplaining your ambition. Let your actions do the talking.

- **Design Your Life Around Growth:** Let your calendar reflect your priorities. Make space for what matters to you — not just what is expected.

Case Study: Dealing with an Abusive Father-in-Law to Building a Thriving Career

"My father-in-law was very abusive. He would play 'nice' in front of others. But—sometimes, he would find me alone and try to force himself on me!" Maya's voice trembled as she sat in an Iron Lady session, tears streaming down her face.

She was not just battling fears; she was drowning in **shame, helplessness, and isolation**.

To the world, her father-in-law was a **respectable man** who smiled warmly in public, spoke with wisdom, and carried the air of a well-respected elder.

But behind closed doors? He was a **predator**.

At first, Maya thought she was imagining it—the way he stood too close, the "accidental" touches, the lingering stares.

Then, one day, when they were alone, he cornered her.

     Chapter 5: Wars in the Family: The 'Double Graduate Maid'

"No one will believe you," he whispered. "You're just a daughter-in-law. Who do you think 'they' will side with?"

Maya felt **trapped.**

She loved her husband deeply.

Her husband was loving but blind to his father's dark side.

Her mother-in-law, bound by tradition, dismissed her concerns with a **chilling indifference—**

"You're imagining things. He's like a father to you."

Fighting back directly would mean a war that she might not be able to win.

So, Maya decided to fight **differently.**

The Mindset Shift – "Control, Not Conflict"

At an **Iron Lady session**, Maya heard something that changed everything:

"Power isn't about fighting harder. It's about controlling the battlefield."

That night, Maya stood in front of the mirror and whispered to herself:

"I will not let him break me. I will play smarter."

Instead of reacting emotionally, she **calculated her moves.**

She knew that a **confrontation** would lead to denial, victim-blaming, and even backlash.

        Chapter 5: Wars in the Family: The 'Double Graduate Maid'

She decided to **change the game.**

The Invisible Defense – "Dismantling the Power Structure"

Maya knew that **abusers thrive in secrecy**.

So, her first move was to shift the power dynamic subtly.

- She started staying in rooms where she was never alone with him.
- She involved more people in daily interactions, ensuring she was never isolated.
- She strengthened her relationships with other family members who respected her, ensuring she had allies.

Suddenly, her father-in-law's **opportunities to trap her became limited.**

And he knew it.

But she did not stop there.

She used **Iron Lady's influence-building techniques** to **control the narrative before he could distort it.**

Controlling the Narrative – "The Power of Perception"

Maya understood that **truth does not always win—perception does.**

She started dropping small, strategic comments **in front of the family**.

- "It's strange; I feel a little uncomfortable alone in my house."

        Chapter 5: Wars in the Family: The 'Double Graduate Maid'

- "I wish everyone in the home respected others!"

She improved her career standing, took on major work projects, and ensured she became much stronger financially.

She was **changing how people saw her**—not as a helpless daughter-in-law but as a **strong, independent woman** with influence.

The result?

Her father-in-law started **sensing the shift.**

He realized that Maya was **no longer alone—that the walls were closing on him.**

That was just the beginning.

The Psychological Trap – "Turning the Pressure Back on Him"

Instead of fighting him head-on, Maya **made him fear exposure.**

- She strategically mentioned a friend who reported abuse and how the abuser's life was ruined.

- She started keeping her phone in recording mode when he was around, letting him see it.

- She made him feel watched.

It worked.

Her father-in-law **grew paranoid.**

His confidence **shattered.**

       Chapter 5: Wars in the Family: The 'Double Graduate Maid'

And then, something surprising happened! **He started avoiding her.**

The predator had become prey.

Without a single fight, Maya had **cornered him into submission.**

Building an Unstoppable Career – "Winning Beyond the Battle"

With the **mental weight lifted**, Maya **thrived** in her career.

- She pitched for a leadership role, using the confidence Iron Lady had instilled in her.

- She established a reputation as a bold and strategic thinker.

- She expanded her network, surrounding herself with powerful women who had walked similar paths.

And what about her marriage?

At first, her husband struggled to **accept the truth.**

But Maya did not **force** him to take sides.

She **let time do the work**—and slowly, as he observed his father's behavior from a new lens, he began to **see it himself.**

He **stood by Maya**, and together, they built a home based on **respect, safety, and equality.**

Their children?

They started **watching their mother lead with power, not fear.**

They learned that **true strength is not about fighting harder but winning smarter.**

The Final Lesson: The Art of Winning without Fighting

Maya's **final words** to women facing similar battles?

"The world teaches women to fight their battles loudly. But true power comes from knowing when to fight and when to make the enemy surrender without a war."

"You don't always need to prove your strength through confrontation. Sometimes, the smartest move is to shift the game so that the battle never happens in the first place."

She did not just **survive**—she **won without fighting.**

5. The Shameless Lady: When Women Dare to Dream Big

Have you ever noticed how a woman who dreams of earning more, aiming higher, or leading boldly is often called *shameless*?

But no one calls a man *shameless* for wanting success.

Because the moment a woman stops apologizing for wanting more, she becomes *dangerous* to the status quo.

6. Reflections: Reclaiming Your Power

Write down the answers to the questions:

1. What are some of the things I have considered as 'normal' on the home front – that are **impacting** me?

2. What is the impact of those in my life on my joy, my growth, and the joy and happiness of people around me?

3. What are one or two of the actions that I can take from now onwards, using ideas and stories from this chapter?

It is time that we questioned ourselves:

Can we ask husbands to be **partners** in their wives' **careers** as well?

     Chapter 5: Wars in the Family: The 'Double Graduate Maid'

Chapter 6: The Battles of a Woman's Mind!

"Is this not a **mistake**? Are you sure you've **shortlisted ME** for the role of **Chief Risk Officer**?" Mamta Shukla asked Anita, the consultant who had just called her.

Even after practicing at Iron Lady for three months, thoroughly preparing herself, and anticipating this moment, she still could not believe it. The call had come, but doubt crept in.

Yet, not only did Mamta go on to **clear the interview**s, but she has been excelling in her new role as Chief Risk Officer!

But this is not just Mamta's story. This is a story that resonates with countless women in the professional world.

Every woman has faced these nagging questions at some point:

- **Am I 'really' ready?**
- **Am I that good?**
- **Am I competent?**
- **Can I really become a CEO?**
- **Am I being selfish?**
- **Am I compromising on my family life?**
- **What if my decisions are wrong at the top?**
- **Is it even possible for ME?**

These questions, when left unanswered, can lead to a constant internal struggle for women.

Following are the constant battles in their minds that constantly women fight:

Ambition vs. Guilt

Duty vs. Self-worth

Confidence vs. Insecurity

Some of these wars in their mind derail women so much – that, combined with the other wars that they need to fight, it almost becomes impossible to deal with for many of them.

We outline below the top 'battles' that women experience in their own minds, the reasons behind these, their impact, and how they can overcome them.

1. The Biggest Fights Are in the Mind

Before the world holds you back—**your mind already has**. It is not just the glass ceilings outside. It is the **invisible cages within**.

Women do not just battle workplace bias or societal pressure. The more profound war is internal. **A quiet,**

relentless struggle that starts long before their first promotion and before their first ambition takes shape.

It manifests as self-doubt when you are about to speak, creeps in as guilt when you prioritize your needs, and paralyzes you with fear when you are ready to take action.

Not because you are incapable. But because you have been conditioned to question your value, to apologize for your ambition, and to *shrink* in moments when you should be *shining*.

That is the actual war within.

Battles in the Mind!

                    Chapter 6: The Battles of a Woman's Mind!

2. Am I Worthy? (Self-worth)

You have just landed a big opportunity, a leadership role, a high-profile project, and a seat at the table. But instead of excitement, doubt creeps in.

So, you downplay your success. You credit luck or the help of others instead of your hard work. You hesitate to take up space, own your expertise, and ask for what you truly deserve.

This is not humility; it is self-doubt. It is holding you back and could also lead to imposter syndrome or self-sabotage.

Did you know:
A **2023 Forbes article** noted that women with imposter syndrome tend to work longer hours to prove themselves, experience more anxiety, and avoid asking for challenging jobs (**75% Of Women Executives Experience Imposter Syndrome**)!

Why Does This Happen?

- **Society Teaches Women to 'Be Modest'**

Girls are told not to boast, be too ambitious, or take credit too openly from an early age. Meanwhile, men are encouraged to 'own' their achievements.

- **Internalized Doubt & Imposter Syndrome**

Due to the constant societal narrative that men are meant to be heroes and women are not, women end up developing internal doubts.

- **Lack of Representation in Leadership**

When you rarely see women in top positions, it becomes harder to envision yourself in a similar role. Without role models, self-doubt takes root.

- **The Fear of Being 'Exposed'**

Women often feel they must prove twice as much to be taken seriously. This pressure makes it seem that every small mistake is a potential disaster.

Impact of Self-worth Struggles

- **The most significant impact of Lack of experiencing worth is Self-sabotage.** You destroy your chances! You end up giving up opportunities that you get. You start believing that you should NOT have so much – that you do a terrible job!

- **You pass on opportunities meant for you – because you assume they deserve more.** You assume you will take more time or more skills or such.

- **You stay stuck** – playing small instead of stepping up. You often do not even want to explore opportunities awaiting you. This becomes a vicious circle!

 Chapter 6: The Battles of a Woman's Mind!

Building Self-worth

Building self-worth is easier than you think! Using a few small tactics, you can make them more quickly!

- ○ **Acknowledge the Internal Battles:**
You have been at war with yourself—doubting, over-explaining, apologizing for taking up space. See it for what it is, and name it. You cannot fight what you do not acknowledge.

- ○ **Challenge Your Beliefs:**
Think back; who told you that 'confidence is arrogance'? Is that ambition selfish? Do you need to 'prove' yourself more than others?

It is time to question those beliefs and understand where they came from.

- ○ **Let It Go:**
It is not enough to wish self-doubt away. Speak to yourself with authority. Tell that voice inside your head: I am NOT a fraud. I belong here. I have earned this. Replacing doubt with affirmations is not cliché—it is strategy.

- ○ **Create Daily Rituals for Confidence:**
Whether you journal your wins, visualize your success, or simply remind yourself of your worth every morning, find habits that fuel your confidence.

- ○ **Recommit to Your Ambitions—Every Day:**
Your dreams do not need validation from anyone but you. Show up for them, day after day. When doubt creeps in,

remind yourself: I am not here by accident. I am here because I worked on it.

The battle may be challenging, but so are you. The moment you **decide to win, you've won** half the battle!

Case Study: The Doubt That Almost Held Me Back

The email was unread for three days.

Ritika had seen the subject line—

"Congratulations on Your Promotion!"

But she found an excuse to do something else whenever she hovered over it: respond to another email, fix a typo in a report, or refill her coffee.

It did not feel real.

She had been with the company for years, outperforming targets, taking on projects no one else wanted, and staying late to clean up the mess she did not create. She had earned this.

So why did it feel like a mistake?

By the time she finally opened the email, her hands were cold. As she read the details—**bigger team, higher pay, a seat at the leadership table**—the voice in her head whispered:

"Maybe, they had no other option."
"Maybe, they think I'm better than I am."
"What if I fail?"

　　　　　　　Chapter 6: The Battles of a Woman's Mind!

She told us about the promotion, but she did not look happy. So, we asked her—

"Why don't you look happy?"

Ritika hesitated,

"I don't know if I deserve it."

We just challenged her gently,

"Have you not spent 3 years working on this? Do you understand how much you are losing every year?"

That hit differently.

She thought about the male colleagues she had mentored, watching them take up space and own their wins without hesitation. She thought about every time she did the work while someone else got the credit.

The following day, something shifted.

When asked about her team's latest project in her first leadership meeting, she caught herself before saying.

"It was a group effort."

Instead, she leaned forward and said,

"I led this initiative, resulting in a **30% efficiency increase**. I am looking at scaling it further across departments."

For the first time, **she did not shrink herself.**

 Chapter 6: The Battles of a Woman's Mind!

A week later, she was asked to lead a company-wide strategy session, and a month later, she was **offered an even bigger opportunity.**

Because this time, she did not sit back and wait to be noticed. She **owned her expertise.**

Women let self-doubt keep them in the shadows while less qualified people take center stage.

3. Should I Speak Up? (Lack of Self-Advocacy)

"I had done all the work. In the end, during the final presentation, I couldn't take credit for my work!"

Sounds familiar?

Women second-guess themselves far more than men. They hesitate, overthink, and wait—hoping their hard work will speak for itself. But it never does. Because in the real world, **visibility beats effort.**

So, while you are double-checking your numbers, rewriting your email for the fifth time, or waiting for someone to notice your contributions, someone else, with half your effort, is already staking their claim.

Chapter 6: The Battles of a Woman's Mind!

Why Does This Happen?

- **Conditioning from Childhood**

Girls are taught to be polite and accommodating, while boys are encouraged to be bold and assertive. This builds hesitation in women when speaking up.

- **Fear of Judgment**

Women fear being labelled aggressive or bossy, leading to self-doubt and second-guessing their ideas.

- **Workplace Bias & Double Standards**

Women face more pushback when self-advocating, while men are often rewarded for the same behaviors.

- **Lack of Role Models & Mentors**

Without visible female leaders, many women struggle to see themselves in positions of authority.

     Chapter 6: The Battles of a Woman's Mind!

What is the Cost of Staying Silent?

Silence is not just about missing one meeting, one project, or one chance to speak up. It builds over time, shaping how you are perceived and, more importantly, how you perceive yourself.

o **Considered introverted or not strategic enough**
The person who speaks up in meetings shares their ideas, makes their presence known, and gets remembered. If you are silent, you risk being considered 'not strategic enough.'

o **Others Getting Credit for Your Ideas**
Did someone repeat what you just said and suddenly get all the credit? It happens because they claimed the space you did not. When you do not own your ideas, someone else will.

o **A Growing Belief That Your Voice Does not Matter**
The more you stay silent, the more it reinforces the belief that your opinions do not hold weight. Over time, this erodes your confidence and makes speaking up even harder.

Building the courage and capability to Speak up!

How can you quickly develop the ability and courage to speak up? Following these steps can help!

o **Recognize the Pattern**
Think back—when was the last time you hesitated to speak up? Was it in a meeting? During a performance review? When did someone take credit for your work?

                         Chapter 6: The Battles of a Woman's Mind!

Recognizing these moments is the first step toward breaking the habit. If you do not see the pattern, you cannot change it.

○ **Reframe Your Inner Dialogue**
That little voice in your head saying, **"What if I'm wrong?"**—challenge it.

Flip the question: **"Can I make a small difference?"**

You do not have to wait till you are 100% sure before speaking up! Own your expertise.

Confidence is not about always knowing the answer but about trusting that your perspective matters.

○ **Take Small, Consistent Steps**
Change may not happen overnight. Start by speaking up in smaller setting-team meetings, one-on-one conversations, and casual discussions. Push yourself to contribute at least one idea in every meeting. The more you practice, the easier it gets.

Speaking up is not arrogance. **It is leadership. Are you ready to claim your space?**

Case study: The Promotion That Never Came!

Tanya mentioned that during her Iron Lady Program,

"I should have the **promotion. I should have been at four levels higher by now.** After **16 years of experience,** my salary is still **six lakh per annum!"**

                     Chapter 6: The Battles of a Woman's Mind!

She said, her voice was steady but laced with frustration,

"But somehow, I have never been promoted."

Tanya was not venting or seeking sympathy; she wanted answers.

After seven years in the same company, with late nights, extra responsibilities, and mentoring new hires, she did everything expected of a high performer. Yet, every promotion cycle felt like déjà vu. She clapped for colleagues moving ahead while she remained stuck.

"I have spoken to my manager and asked for feedback. They always say, 'You're doing great; just keep at it.' But when the time comes, it is always someone else who gets promoted."

The worst sting? A junior she had trained got promoted over her. When she congratulated him, he admitted,

"I thought you'd be next."

That night, staring at her reflection on a dark screen, she wondered, **"Am I just not leadership material?"**

Her story is not unique. Countless women hit this invisible wall—told to 'keep working hard' while others leap ahead. But through Iron Lady, Tanya learned the truth—hard work is not rewarded if no one sees it.

She made changes. Instead of waiting for validation, she highlighted her achievements. She stopped downplaying her contributions.

 Chapter 6: The Battles of a Woman's Mind!

One day, during a discussion with her boss, instead of staying quiet, she spoke up:

"I'm happy to report that I've completed a department-wise project, saving 10 hours of work each week per FTE. I'd like to understand how to get a bigger opportunity and move to the next level."

Her manager looked surprised. For the first time, Tanya was not just doing the work—she was claiming credit.

Her manager raised an eyebrow.

"You've never spoken this confidently before, Tanya."

She said-

"That's changing,"

A few weeks later, she was leading a significant project, and **two months later**, she **got the promotion**.

Because this time, she was not waiting to be recognized—she was shamelessly pitching what she had already earned.

Self-doubt keeps women in the shadows while less qualified people take center stage.

<u>Did you know:</u>
Men apply for promotions when they meet **60%** of the criteria. Women wait until they meet **100%,** according to Harvard Business Review.

Stop waiting. Start speaking up, one sentence at a time!

4. I Need to Do Things Perfectly! (Perfectionism and guilt)

You rewrite that email five times before hitting send. You tweak your presentation slides a little more—because they are not perfect yet. You overthink every detail, afraid that a tiny flaw will ruin everything.

When something is not up to your impossibly high standards? That tiny mistake haunts you. You tell yourself you should have done better.

Perfectionism can feel like a strength – it makes you meticulous, hardworking, and thorough.

At the same time, it may also get you stuck! Holding you back from moving ahead.

What is the Cost of Perfectionism and Guilt

○ **Missed Opportunities**

You hesitate too long, waiting for the perfect moment, and someone else leaps before you do. You hold back from applying for that promotion, speaking up in meetings, or launching that project because it is

"Not ready yet."

 Chapter 6: The Battles of a Woman's Mind!

- **Chronic Stress and Burnout**

It is not only exhausting but also unsustainable. You pour endless energy into making everything flawless, leaving yourself drained, overwhelmed, and frustrated. And the worst part? You rarely feel satisfied with your results.

- **Fear of Failure Stops Growth**

It makes you avoid risks. You do not take on challenging projects or leadership roles because you fear making mistakes. You stick to what feels safe, even when it limits your potential.

- **Never Feeling 'Good Enough'**

No matter how much you achieve, you still feel like you could have done more and better. The goalpost keeps moving, making success feel unattainable. You do not celebrate wins—you analyze what could have been improved.

Why Does This Happen?

- **Fear of Judgment**

Women are often judged more harshly than men in the workplace. So, we overcompensate, trying to be flawless to avoid criticism.

- **Childhood Conditioning**

Women grow up hearing,

> **"Be a good girl," or "Do it right or don't do it at all."**

　　　　　Chapter 6: The Battles of a Woman's Mind!

This plants the idea that anything less than perfection is a failure.

- **High Expectations in Every Role**

Society expects women to excel in everything—work, home, parenting, and relationships. So, we internalize this pressure and hold ourselves to impossible standards.

Overcoming perfection and guilt

- **Redefine Success**

Perfection is a myth. Instead of asking, "Is this perfect?" ask, "Is this effective?" High achievers do not waste time chasing perfection; they focus on making an impact. **Done** is better than **perfect**.

- **Take Imperfect Action**

Challenge yourself to send that email after two drafts, not five. Speak up in a meeting without rehearsing every word. Apply for that opportunity even if you do not meet 100% of the requirements. Actions build confidence, waiting kills it.

- **Celebrate Progress**

Shift your mindset from

"I should have done better" to "It's getting better!"

Chapter 6: The Battles of a Woman's Mind!

Recognize small wins, appreciate your efforts, and remind yourself that growth comes from learning and not getting everything right.

It does not make you better; it keeps you stuck. The real power is showing up, speaking up, and taking action—even when it is not perfect.

Case Study: The Flaw That Almost Killed Her Business

Aarini stared at the product samples on her desk. Rows of handcrafted candles, each labeled, each carefully poured. But her eyes kept landing on one—the wick slightly off-center, the scent not as strong as she wanted.

It was not perfect.

She picked it up and turned it over, debating whether to throw it out. It did not matter that she had spent months perfecting the formula, refining branding, and agonizing over every detail. One flaw was that it felt like everything was wrong.

This was not just about a candle.

The night before launching her website, she rewrote product descriptions ten times, tweaking words and adjusting images. Her competitors went live with half the effort. They moved forward. She stayed frozen, editing, re-editing, and convincing herself it was not ready.

When customers placed orders, she panicked. What if they noticed imperfections? A typo in a marketing post ruined her day. A tiny air bubble in the wax? She would redo the entire batch.

Perfectionism was not improving her business—it was stalling it.

'Letting go' was not easy.

At first, she fought it.

As she practiced the **Iron Lady Way**, she started reminding herself,

"Done is more important than perfect."

She forced herself to launch the website—despite wanting to tweak one more thing.

And then, the orders came in.

At first, it was thrilling. Until a customer messaged:

"Love the scent! But the wick burns unevenly."

Aarini spiraled. She wanted to recall the batch.

But then she noticed something.

The same customer had left a five-star review.

That moment did not fix her. But it planted a seed.

                    Chapter 6: The Battles of a Woman's Mind!

Over the next few months, she made minor changes, set deadlines—no endless revisions, and released products before they felt "ready."

It was not easy.

Some days, she hovered over the Post button for an eternity. Resisted the urge to scrap batches. But she reminded herself:

Perfectionism did not make her business better. It held it back.

One evening, months later, she picked up a candle with a slightly off-center wick.

Before, she would have tossed it.

This time, she packed it in a customer's order.

And closed the box.

Without a second thought.

5. Reflections: The Shameless Lady

Women's toughest battles are not in boardrooms but in their minds.

Self-doubt, guilt, imposter syndrome, and perfectionism keep many from reaching their full power.

But are these struggles indeed theirs to carry? Or are they conditioned beliefs that need to be challenged?

Chapter 6: The Battles of a Woman's Mind!

The Shameless Lady needs to speak up. Know and express her worth.

She is the woman who walks into the room and owns it—even when her knees are shaking.

She is the one who speaks up, asks for what she wants, and dares to say,

"I deserve this."

The world may call her names. Too loud. Too much. Too ambitious. But she knows the truth: They call you shameless when you stop being easily ignored.

Write down the answers below:

1. What silent battles in my mind keep me from taking up challenges?

2. What is the impact of these in my life on my confidence, my income, and my progress in my life?

  Chapter 6: The Battles of a Woman's Mind!

3. What is one step that I can take today, based on the ideas from this chapter to be more powerful?

It is time to break free from the doubts and expectations that hold you back.

We do not need a world with '**Perfect Women.**'

We need a world where women are encouraged to be **Shameless**!

Chapter 7: Shakti

"Each of us is blessed with 'enormous **Shakti**.' It's up to us how we use it!" as she narrated her story, Girija mentioned how she reached the top and earned a **crore-plus yearly income**!

Most women do not understand their own '**Shakti.**'

They believe they possess some basic skills, strengths, and knowledge, as well as certain technical skills.

They continue to develop these basic skills and knowledge.

Basic certifications, courses, and learning do not enable them to nurture and harness their own 'Shakti' completely.

They end up hearing comments like:

- You are not strategic enough.
- You need to be more assertive and more extroverted.
- Your executive presence needs work.

They start to wonder, 'They are right. I don't have the natural leadership traits.'

Before you fully grasp the concept of Shakti, the first step is to understand the strengths required at each level of leadership

At every level, a new set of strengths is needed.

Let us examine the strengths required at various levels of leadership.

1. Strengths at Different Levels

Success in any career is about developing and demonstrating **the right strengths at the right time**. What gets you ahead at one stage will not necessarily keep you ahead at the next.

Let us break down the **key strengths needed at each stage.**

Level 1: Basic Level (Junior Roles) – Excelling at Tasks

At the start of your career, success is largely determined by how effectively **you execute tasks**. It is less about leadership and more about **reliability, accuracy, and efficiency**.

Your ability to follow instructions, meet deadlines, and produce quality work is what gets you noticed.

This stage involves demonstrating that you can be trusted with responsibilities. You are building your **expertise in specific skills and tools,** learning how things work, and getting comfortable with workplace expectations.

What this looks like in action:

- Complete assigned work with attention to detail and deliver on time.
- Following guidelines, instructions, and established processes carefully.
- Developing expertise in specific tools, systems, or tasks relevant to your role.

At this stage, your job is not about making big

Chapter 7: Shakti

decisions or leading teams but about **being dependable and consistently delivering great work**. Think of it as being a strong team player.

Your role is to perform well, contribute effectively, and **build the foundation for future growth**.

Level 2: Mid-Level (Managerial Roles) – Leading People & Processes

At this stage, success is about what you do and **how well you manage others and improve workflows**. The challenge is shifting from **doing the work yourself** to **getting the work done through others**.

This is where problem-solving, delegation, and collaboration become essential.

You must balance individual contributions with team leadership, ensuring people and processes run smoothly. It is no longer about excelling at tasks but enabling others to perform at their best.

What this looks like in action:

- Manage a team or a process and ensure it runs effectively.
- Making decisions that improve productivity, efficiency, and outcomes.
- Delegating tasks while providing guidance and support.
- Balancing hands-on work with leadership responsibilities.

The strengths you develop here determine how well you drive progress and set yourself up for leadership.

Level 3: Top-Level (Leadership & Executive Roles) – Driving Strategy, work with a 'purpose' and Big Goals

At the highest levels, the focus shifts towards creating and driving a **purpose. It is about performance at scale** and projecting and achieving 'Big Goals.'

We call these the 3 **P**s of leadership:

- **P**urpose
- **P**erformance at Scale
- **P**rojection of your leadership / brand / influence

Leaders at this level drive change, **influence people and make high-impact decisions** that shape the organization's future.

Success at this level is about **long-term thinking, innovation, and decisions that move the organization forward.**

It is about navigating uncertainty, aligning teams with a larger vision, and dealing with complex organizational dynamics.

What this looks like in action:

Purpose

- Creating, communicating, and driving a specific 'purpose,' communicating powerfully with stakeholders.
- Inspiring teams and stakeholders to align with a larger purpose.
- Creating teams / leaders to drive the purpose ahead.

Performance

- Exceptional performance with the least effort / time.
- Defining strategies and tactics and delivering those.
- Communicating the Big Goals and getting them done.

Projection

- Projecting the Purpose, projecting your ideas, projecting your ideas.
- Making high-stakes decisions that shape the future of the organization or department.
- Handling complex organizational politics and understanding market positioning.

Even in **specialist roles,** such as doctors or niche technologists, understanding the driving 3 Ps of leadership enables one to excel.

Women who recognize and build the strengths required at each stage grow faster to the top. The key is to **adapt, evolve, and develop** the capabilities that leadership demands.

Growing at every stage is not just about **what you do** but **how you do it**—which comes down to strength. But strength is not one-dimensional. It is not just about technical expertise or leadership presence.

                     Chapter 7: Shakti

2. Your sources of Strengths

Where do these strengths come from?

We explore the **three core sources** of strengths:

- A. **Personal Strengths** (Character / personality-driven)
    - o **Body** (Action and Execution)
    - o **Mind** (Strategy and Innovation)
    - o **Heart** (Energy, Emotion, and People Skills)

- B. **Functional Strengths** (Mastery of skills & expertise)

- C. **Industry-Related Strengths** (Domain knowledge & leadership)

a. Personal Strengths: Your Inner Powerhouse

Personal strengths are the **core qualities that shape how you work, think, and lead.**

They define your **natural tendencies, problem-solving approaches, and leadership style.**

These strengths are divided into three essential dimensions: **body, mind, and heart.**

- o **Body (Action and Execution) – The Power of Doing**

Chapter 7: Shakti

Your bodily strength is the **engine that drives execution**, and it rests on three pillars: **Discipline, Diligence, and Deployment.**

Discipline

This is the foundation of **consistency**. It lets you stay committed to your goals despite distractions, setbacks, or obstacles. Women who master discipline create **structured routines** that make productivity **non-negotiable**. Instead of relying on motivation alone, they **build systems** that ensure execution.

Example: Anika, Operations Manager

Anika was known for getting things done efficiently. When her team struggled with meeting deadlines, she implemented strict **time-blocking**, created a **goal-tracking system**, and held herself accountable through **daily progress checks**. Within six months, project completion rates increased by **40 percent**, setting a new standard for the company.

Diligence

This is the **ability to persist through challenges**. It means maintaining high effort even when things do not go as planned. Women who embody diligence **do not quit at the first sign of failure**; they analyse, adapt, and try again.

Case Study: Kavita, IT Project Manager

Kavita was tasked with leading a significant **software migration project** that faced multiple roadblocks. Despite resistance from stakeholders and unexpected technical issues, she **methodically problem-solved**, consulted experts, and kept the team motivated. The project was completed **three weeks before schedule**, earning her a **leadership award**.

Deployment

This is the **art of taking action and using resources**. Women who excel at deployment do not overthink; they **take bold action, use resources smartly, and refine along the way**. They ensure that ideas move from **strategy to execution**, making them high-impact leaders.

Case Study: Sonali Sagar, Founder, Symphony Software

Sonali had a brilliant **business idea for an application platform.** Instead of spending months perfecting a plan, she **launched a prototype within 30 days**, gathered feedback, and iterated. Within a year, her company reached multicrore in revenue and became **profitable**.

- **Mind (Strategy & Innovation) – The Power of Thinking**

Strategic thinking **separates leaders from followers**. It is about looking beyond daily tasks and **seeing the bigger picture**. Women with strategic strength do not just react—they **anticipate trends, identify opportunities, and create long-term value.** They ask, 'What is next? What is possible?'

                                    Chapter 7: Shakti

Case Study: Priya, Marketing Director

Priya noticed her company was **losing younger customers**. Instead of waiting for leadership to see the decline, she **proactively analysed market trends** and proposed an app-first **strategy**. Despite initial scepticism, her campaigns went viral, increasing brand engagement by **200 percent in six months**.

Women who develop strategic thinking dedicate time to industry research, simplify their strategies, and constantly look for ways to multiply their impact.

- **Heart (Energy, Emotion & People Skills) – The Power of Connection**

Women who master this strength know how to **motivate, influence, and create strong team cultures**. They do not just drive results; they **build trust, handle conflict, and drive collaboration**.

Case Study: Aisha, VP of Engineering – Rebuilding the team.

Aisha took over a team with **low morale and high turnover**. She rebuilt trust by **listening, implementing recognition programs, and creating clear career paths**. Engagement rose 40% in six months, and turnover dropped **60%**. Her **approach** transformed a struggling team into a high-performing one.

A strong, heart-centred leader balances **empathy with boundaries**, ensuring she leads with **compassion and clarity**.

b. Functional Strengths: Mastering Your Craft

Functional strengths are the **technical and domain-specific skills** that differentiate high performers. Mastering your functional strengths means **being exceptional at your work** and **continuously upgrading your expertise**.

Case Study: Sneha, HR Leader – Driving Business Impact Through HR

Sneha transformed HR from a **support function to a business driver** by aligning people strategies with revenue goals. She **linked workforce productivity to financial outcomes**, proving that **engaged teams boosted profitability**. By presenting HR as a **profit enabler,** not just a cost centre, she secured leadership buy-in for key initiatives. Her **business-first approach** led to her fast-tracking as CHRO.

Women who stand out in their careers **innovate, optimize, and add value beyond expectations**, using their functional strengths.

c. Industry-Related Strengths: Navigating the Bigger Picture

Industry-related strengths involve **understanding the trends, regulations, and challenges unique to your field**. Women who cultivate this strength become **go-to experts, influencing decision-making and driving change**.

Chapter 7: Shakti

Case Study: Mita, Healthcare Executive

Mita used her **deep understanding of FDA regulations** to expedite **product approvals** for her med-tech company. She became the **go-to leader for global expansions**, significantly increasing the company's market reach.

Women who excel in this area attend industry events, contribute to **thought leadership**, and build credibility by **staying ahead** of emerging trends.

3. Your roadmap to Excel using your Strengths.

Leaders win by combining strengths—the **harmonious blend of personal, functional, and industry strengths**.

Women who stand out in leadership **do not operate in silos**; they **integrate their strengths strategically**.

Step 1: Strengthen, Elevate, and Showcase Your Strengths

- **Strengthen:** Identify your **strongest skills** and continuously develop them.

- **Elevate:** Position yourself as an **expert** or a **specialist** by taking on high-impact projects and sharing your knowledge.

- **Tactics:** Develop tactics that use your strengths, making you a winner. Understand what you can accomplish.

- **Showcase:** Speak up about your **achievements** in meetings, industry panels, and online platforms.

Step 2: Manage and Hide Your Weaknesses

- **Manage:** If a weakness is holding you back, **learn enough to minimize its impact**. Also, allies and support systems should be found to manage the weaknesses.

- **Hide:** Delegate tasks **not in your zone of genius**, and **do not dwell on areas that do not define your success**.

- **Note:** we have had many experiences where women **'honestly' admitted** their weaknesses and their careers were destroyed. Never let this happen to you!

Women who integrate their strengths do not just **advance their careers**; they **redefine leadership itself**.

4. Your Shakti (Hidden Superpowers!)

Once you understand the sources of your strengths, how do you build an exponential growth path that leverages something beyond all your strengths?

Through **Shakti**!

Shakti, the **divine feminine energy,** is not just a concept—it is a tangible force that women can harness to **lead, innovate, and win**.

                              Chapter 7: Shakti

The Shakti!

When you understand and nurture your **Shakti** fully – you develop **formidable real-world strengths**.

Women who succeed in leadership strategically leverage their 'Shakti' to solve problems, influence people and drive results.

Shakti: The Superpowers You Can Harness!

Since your childhood, you've carried three extraordinary Shakti.

Chapter 7: Shakti

- **The Fierce Personal Shakti**
- **The Shakti of Your Surroundings and Absorption**
- **The Strategic Shakti of Knowledge & Experience**

You may not have named them so far. You didn't even realise you were using some them already.

They've shaped every decision, every breakthrough, every quiet rebellion.

The only problem?
You were trained to ignore them.
Taught to distrust them.

It's time to call them what they are: **Your Superpowers.**

It's time to use them—boldly, deliberately, shamelessly.

a. Shakti 1: The Fierce Personal Shakti

This is the raw fire that once burned freely in you—before the filters kicked in.
The confidence that let you speak without fear.
The instinct that guided you without overthinking.
The energy that pushed you to try, fail, and rise again—without shame.

As you grew older, that power was ignored.
And so, you toned it down.

But here's the truth: That version of you never left. She's just waiting for you to let her lead again.

                                        Chapter 7: Shakti

One step to Nurture your Fierce Personal Shakti:

- Take one action based on your old forgotten confidence this week!

b. Shakti 2: The Shakti of Your Surroundings and Absorption

You are not just observant—you absorb!

You notice tension before it's acknowledged. You pick up on tone, body language, and power shifts.
You decode politics without needing the playbook.

This ability to absorb, adapt, and intuit is not a sign of weakness—it's a strategic advantage.

While most women have this Shakti, few *leverage* it.
You see the patterns but hesitate to act on them.

One step to Nurture this Shakti:

- Visualize yourself taking one action – using the power and strengths of someone around you. Take one small action to imbibe that strength yourself.

c. Shakti 3: The Strategic Shakti of Knowledge & Experience

You've studied, observed, practiced, delivered.

You've led projects, solved crises, navigated politics, and held it all together—often without being noticed.

However, while you've gained both knowledge and experience, you've been taught to speak only when you're certain.

This belief—that you need to know more before you can lead—is a lie. **You already do.**

Your knowledge gives you clarity.
Your experience gives you foresight.
Together, they give you power most people *never* reach.

It's time to use it—not subtly, but strategically.

One step to Nurture this Shakti:

Frame your next contribution with "From experience…" or "Here's what I've seen work…"—and let it land with weight.

Case study: On the verge of losing her job, she becomes the 'Leader of the pack!'

Hema was put on a **performance improvement plan**—one step away from losing her job.

She was stunned. All her life, she had been a **brilliant performer**. Just six months ago, she had been **promoted** to a higher role, a testament to her **hard work and results**. She continued to put in the same effort, delivering at the same level.

                                Chapter 7: Shakti

So why was she suddenly being seen as a **non-performer**?

Confused and frustrated, she asked her boss what had changed. The response shook her.

"Expectations are **way higher** now. You're in a **bigger** role."

Hema had assumed that the strengths that got her here—her ability to execute and deliver results—would be enough. But as she went through the Iron Lady program, she realized something critical:

She had **miscalculated**.

Her role had changed, but her approach had not. She needed to develop **new strengths** that aligned with her new responsibilities.

Hema started looking at her work differently.

She went through specific activities to nurture and leverage her **Shakti**!

Through various daily and weekly activities, she started realizing the Shakti and developing her strengths and skills using those.

She shifted from just executing tasks to leading, influencing, and **making strategic decisions**. She took ownership of bigger-picture thinking, aligning her work with **business goals** rather than just task completion.

She began to **speak up in leadership meetings**, contribute ideas beyond her immediate role, and position herself as a **problem solver rather than just a doer**.

Within a few months, **her performance skyrocketed**. Not only did she meet the expectations set in her improvement plan, but she exceeded them.

One day, in an Iron Lady session, she reflected:

> "I had never realized I had so much of **Shakti** within. The moment I did, I became **far more capable quickly**."

Her **confidence grew, and so did her impact**. Her boss, who once doubted her ability to succeed in the new role, now saw her as a **key decision-maker**.

By the end of the performance improvement period, **she had secured her position, led critical projects, and mentored others**.

Looking back, Hema realized that **success was not just about working harder—it was about working smarter, evolving, and embracing the strengths that genuinely mattered at each growth stage**.

5. Reflections

Each one of us has an enormous **'Shakti'** within.

1. List at least three of your strengths below:

                              Chapter 7: Shakti

2. Consider how you can apply these concepts to Level 3 based on the information in **this chapter.** Write down a few small steps that you can take to strengthen the above strengths.

3. Write down 2-3 of your weaknesses.

4. Write down a few actions you'll take to manage these weaknesses. Remember not to expose this weakness unnecessarily anywhere!

'Shameless Ladies' are willing to acknowledge their **'Shakti'** – nurture them and WIN.

They understand their weaknesses but are not bogged down by the weaknesses!

A community that **truly** celebrates the strengths of women in the various 'avatars' of Shakti, is a happy community.

Are you ready to CELEBRATE your Shakti and bring them to the foreground?

                    Chapter 7: Shakti

Chapter 8: The Tactics: Win Without Fighting

"Thanks to these **tactics**, I've **reached the top**," mentioned **Rajani Ramachandra**, Transformational Change Specialist and a Role model within the **Iron Lady Army**.

Over the last few years, we have designed a set of Winning Tactics that enable women to overcome the most demanding challenges and reach the top.

These **twenty-seven tactics** together are called the **Iron Lady Way**.

This chapter dives into four of these tactics.

Over the last seven years, we have experienced that women who master these tactics from the Iron Lady Way grow much faster in their careers or businesses.

Ready? Let us dive in.

1. The Shameless Pitch

Claim Your Seat with **Strategic Audacity**

When we ask women,

"Are you ready to pitch for the role of CEO?"

The most common response is,

If not for the role of CEO, what about **pitching** for the **next promotion**?

What about **pitching** and negotiating for a **BIG hike**?

How about the next role?

What about negotiating to **hire a maid**?

No?

This hesitation is one of the key reasons why capable women often miss leadership roles.

**SHE DIDN'T PLAY BY THEIR RULES.
SHE REWROTE THE GAME.**

You need always to keep this in mind:

You get what you **negotiate for**. Not what you **deserve**.

The Shameless Pitch, a tactic created at Iron Lady and now mastered by thousands of Iron Ladies, empowers women to demand the roles, resources, and recognition they deserve.

Women who master this accomplish big goals faster.

The Shameless Pitch is **not** just about – **just being bullish**!

It is mastering the **HOW** and **WHAT** of the Shameless Pitch that matters!

a. The **HOW** of Shameless Pitch

Before you begin to start your pitch, get prepared with the mindset and the methods.

There are **four pillars** of **HOW**.

i.   Showcase 'YES-Worthy' – Own Your worth (Past + Future)

Showcasing **"YES-worthy"** means behaving with the confidence that you deserve 'it' (whatever you pitch for)—not just because of past achievements, but because you are ready to deliver future results.

Too often, women focus on why they are NOT ready instead of why they are ready!

It is in how you come across, your body language, and your entire presence!

- **Example:**

Maria, a mid-level manager, pitched her promotion by saying,

"I increased revenue by 30%, and my strategy for the next quarter can drive another 25% growth."

She made her case compelling by showcasing her 'yes worthiness' and her future impact alongside past wins.

- **Try this:**

    Create a "brag sheet" with key achievements and a 90-day action plan for your desired role.

- **Avoid this:**

    Waiting for someone to **"notice"** your worth. Pitch yourself—proactively.

ii.   Be 'No-Ready' – Prepare Counteroffers

Rejections happen. The key is to expect them and be ready to pivot – emotionally and tactically.

Many women take **"no"** as the definitive answer, while successful professionals treat it as an opening for negotiation.

                    Chapter 8: The Tactics: Win Without Fighting

- **Example:**

Priya was rejected for a leadership role. Instead of backing down, she asked:

> "If this role isn't available now, **could I lead the upcoming regional expansion** as a pilot?"

Six months later, she got promoted.

- **Use this script:**

> "If [X] isn't possible, could we explore [Y]?"

Six months later, she got promoted. Instead of accepting rejection, she kept the conversation open by saying:

> "If a leadership role isn't possible right now, could we explore me leading the upcoming regional expansion as a trial?"

- **Avoid this:**

Walking away after a "no." Always have counteroffers.

### iii.	Pitch with Intent and Energy

Your message is important, but how you deliver it matters just as much. Many women unintentionally weaken their pitch by using hesitant language like

"I just think..." or "Maybe we could..."

These phrases make statements sound uncertain rather than confident. A strong pitch needs three things: confidence, clarity, and conviction.

- **Example:**

Tech Leader Lena pitched her AI project like this:

"This will reduce costs by 15% and position us as market leaders. Let us start the pilot next week."

Notice the difference? No **"maybes" or "just"**! Only decisive action.

- **Tactic:**

Replace soft language with assertive phrases:

Instead of **"Maybe we could try…,"** say **"I recommend we move forward with…"**

Removing hesitant words like "maybe" and "could" makes your statement more decisive and persuasive.

- **Avoid this:**

Letting nerves weaken your delivery. Practice power poses beforehand.

iv. **Deploy Smart Tactics – Timing, Visibility, and Environment.**

Even the best pitch can fall flat if delivered at the wrong time or to the wrong audience. Smart pitchers know when and how to make their ask.

        Chapter 8: The Tactics: Win Without Fighting

- **Timing is key:**

Time your pitch wisely. The best moments are right after a significant achievement, like closing a big deal, or during budget planning when decisions about resources and roles are being made.

- **Get noticed:**

Take initiative by joining high-visibility projects that showcase your skills. Keep your work noticed by sending monthly updates highlighting your key achievements.

- **Example:**

After closing a **$2 million deal,** a sales professional saw the perfect opportunity to ask for a leadership role. Instead of waiting, she leveraged her recent success to prove her value.

By making the request when her impact was most visible, she increased her chances of getting a **"yes."** Her timing made it impossible for decision-makers to ignore her contribution and potential.

- **Avoid this:**

Pitching in a rushed or public setting. Choose a private, focused moment to make your case.

b. The <u>WHAT</u> of Shameless Pitches: Content That Gets a YES!

Once you have mastered the <u>**HOW,**</u> you are ready for the actual content and communication.

The three following pillars of the Shameless Pitch show you the content.

1. Find and Solve <u>THEIR</u> Problems – Align with Their Needs

Decision-makers care about their goals—which may not be <u>yours</u>. Yet, many women make pitches centred on their needs instead of showing how to solve a problem.

- **Example:**

A marketing director successfully secured budget approval by aligning her request with the CEO's goal. She framed it as a solution, saying:

"This investment will increase digital outreach by 40 percent, directly driving revenue."

Because her proposal addressed a key business priority, it was approved immediately.

- **Try this:**

Instead of just making a request, connect it to what matters most to the decision-maker.

"I know [X challenge] is a priority. Here's how I can solve it."

2. Differentiation – Why 'You' or 'your service' differ.

Your skills, personality, and vision make you unique. However, many women hesitate to highlight their strengths.

Instead of simply saying, **"I work hard,"** show the value you bring.

- **Example:**

A finance manager secured a director role by clearly expressing her **differentiation** as below.

"I don't just handle finance—I deliver exceptional <u>business value and growth</u>."

- **Avoid:**

Avoid vague and generic statements that fail to effectively highlight your actual value. Instead, be specific about your strengths and the impact you bring.

Avoid saying things like "I work hard."

3. Make an <u>irresistible</u> Offer

The best pitches offer a low-risk, high-reward, **immediate** outcome. Make it easy for decision-makers to say yes.

- **Example:**

Decision-makers are more likely to approve requests when they immediately see clear benefits with minimal risk. Instead of just asking, offer a measurable outcome.

          Chapter 8: The Tactics: Win Without Fighting

"I propose a 90-day pilot to test this strategy. If client retention improves by 15 percent, we can move forward with my promotion."

Pair your request with something valuable in return:

"I'll lead the client onboarding process if I receive the necessary training and resources."

This approach makes approval easier and positions you as a problem-solver.

c. Final Word: Pitch Like an Iron Lady

A **Shameless Pitch** is not arrogance—it is strategic audacity.

Start small: negotiate a project, then a promotion.

Every yes builds momentum.

Now, get that **yes**!

d. Case Study: How a finance manager pitched for a director role

Sarah is a finance professional with **15 years of experience**. She is applying for the role of Finance Director at a mid-sized tech company. But her journey has not been without hurdles.

For years, Sarah had watched less experienced colleagues leap ahead. She had been the silent force behind major financial wins—streamlining budgets, increasing cash flow efficiency, and identifying hidden revenue opportunities.

Yet, when promotions were handed out, her name was rarely in the conversation.

At first, she rationalized it.

"Maybe I need to work harder. Maybe next year."

But deep down, she knew the truth. She was not being overlooked because she lacked skills—she was being ignored because she had not **pitched herself** as the leader she already was.

The moment that shattered her self-doubt came at a performance review meeting. Sarah had walked in expecting recognition for her contributions—after all, she had saved the company millions in financial restructuring.

Instead, her manager's words cut deep,

"You've done great work, Sarah, but we see you as an excellent executor, not necessarily a leader."

It was not just the words—it was the implication.

For years, she had assumed that hard work alone would propel her forward. But **execution was not enough. Leadership had to be claimed.**

She left the meeting feeling like all those extra hours, strategic decisions, and financial successes had been reduced to nothing more than **'supporting' work.** She was tired of waiting for someone to recognize her leadership.

		Chapter 8: The Tactics: Win Without Fighting

Sarah enrolled in Iron Lady's leadership program, and for the first time, she saw her hesitation for what it was—a **fear of claiming her space.**

She understood how to value her worth, anticipate rejection, and pitch her ideas confidently.

Even with all the tactics, the success did not come immediately.

She caught herself falling into old habits—working harder, delivering more, hoping someone would notice. But now, she recognized the pattern.

Sarah practiced with her mentors. The fear of rejection still loomed. She prepared her pitch multiple times and got ready.

The only way forward was to pitch, even if it felt uncomfortable.

When the time came, Sarah did not wait for the perfect moment—she created it.

She had faced setbacks, moments of doubt, and times when recognition felt out of reach. But she did not let that stop her.

She scheduled a meeting with the **CFO and CEO**, framing it as a **"Finance Strategy Discussion."** Instead of sitting back and waiting for validation.

She took control:

   Chapter 8: The Tactics: Win Without Fighting

"I have been leading high-impact financial strategies for years. But I am here to do more than **manage the company's finances—I am keen to drive business growth**. I am ready to take on the Finance Director role to deliver even greater results."

She spoke with conviction, without hedging or hesitation.

She did not ask—she owned the space.

Three weeks later, Sarah received the offer letter.

The CFO later told her,

"We always knew you were capable, but this pitch sealed it. You didn't just say you deserved it—you proved why the company needed you in that seat."

Sarah's story is proof that talent alone is not enough. Opportunities do not just appear—you must claim them.

However, even after learning the tactics, she still had to overcome her hesitation. Her biggest win was not the promotion—it was overcoming her fear of asking for it.

Her biggest lesson?

Success does not come quickly. If you are doing the work, you should be getting the title. But no one hands it over unless you step up and pitch for it.

2. Crucibles of Leadership

Building Childlike Belief with the maturity of an adult!

 Chapter 8: The Tactics: Win Without Fighting

As leaders, we must inspire and **instil a sense of belief** in others.

When we asked our **5-year-old daughter,** what do you want to become when you grow up, she mentioned,

"I want to be a **doctor, an engineer, a dentist, a mother, and a boss!"**

At five years old, we believe we can conquer the world.

As we grow up, we are often taught to be **"good girls,"** which shapes our self-perception. Questions like **"Am I ready?" and "Do I deserve this?"** start to hold us back.

These doubts hold women from stepping up, taking charge, and confidently leading.

However, this is not about returning to who you were as a child—it's about **creating beliefs** that genuinely empower you and inspire others to do the same.

The **three-step** method ahead has helped thousands of women recreate their beliefs and inspire their children and teams to believe much more.

Now, it is your turn!

 Chapter 8: The Tactics: Win Without Fighting

Let go, Bring Forth and Commit!

Disclaimer:

Apply these tactics under expert guidance. People who are undergoing **psychological challenges** should refrain from doing these without the guidance of an expert or a psychologist.

  Chapter 8: The Tactics: Win Without Fighting

Step 1: LET GO

Sometimes, even the most minor incidents or experiences can create doubt in your mind.

Following the three-step methodology below enables you to recreate and CHOOSE beliefs intentionally rather than 'accidentally.'

Let go (release) What Weighs You Down: disempowering beliefs, resentments, anger, etc.

Methodology: Identify and release resentment, self-doubt, fear of judgment, and disempowering beliefs. **Any small thing** that holds you back.

Rituals to Practice:

- **The Burn & Breathe:** Write one limiting belief ("I'm not powerful enough," "I am not good enough") or resentment on paper. Burn it (safely), then take five deep breaths. Say aloud: "This no longer serves me."

- **The Accountability Mirror:** Stand in front of a mirror and name one inhibition you released that day. "Today, I let go of needing everyone's approval."

- **Example:**

Maria had faced workplace discrimination and often thought, "I don't belong here." This belief held her back—until she

                    Chapter 8: The Tactics: Win Without Fighting

decided to challenge it. She took a bold step and volunteered
to lead a high-stakes project she had once avoided.

The outcome? She gained clarity, confidence, and the space
to reach her full potential.

Step 2: BRING FORTH

Reignite Your Childlike Energy and Belief!

Methodology: Declare with a lot of power and energy, "I
BRING FORTH XXXXXXXXX," whether it is joy, curiosity,
energy, a sense of belief, or creativity.

Rituals to Practice:

- **The Joy Sprint:** Do something for 2 minutes to energize
  yourself: dance, sketch, sing badly. No purpose, no
  rules.

- **The Accountability Mirror:** Stand in front of a mirror
  and make a powerful declaration: "I BRING FORTH
  XXXXXXXXX," whatever is most exciting for you.

- **Example:**

Priya, a naturally introverted engineer, struggled with
expressing herself confidently. To change this, she started a
simple two-minute morning ritual—affirming,

                Chapter 8: The Tactics: Win Without Fighting

"I bring energy into my communication."

Over time, this tiny habit transformed how she showed up at work. Her renewed confidence led her to pitch an innovative design, which earned her a leadership role.

The result? A powerful presence that drew others in and made them believe in her vision.

Step 3: COMMIT

Commit to a new Belief / intention / goal.

Methodology: Declare your commitment with intention and energy:

"I commit to [your intention / goal]."

This simple yet powerful statement shifts belief into action. Say it with conviction, then follow through with unwavering focus. When you commit unapologetically, you create momentum, build resilience, and turn your vision into reality.

Rituals to Practice:

- **The Power Pact**
  Write your dream ("I commit to accomplish my dreams.") and read it aloud while standing in a power pose.

- **The Accountability Mirror:** Stand in front of a mirror and make a powerful declaration: "I commit to XXXXXXXXXX," whatever you intend to commit to.

- **Example:**

Fatima grew up with a scarcity mindset, constantly feeling like wealth was out of reach. To change that, she started a simple daily ritual—writing down,

"I commit to being rich."

This practice rewired her mindset, giving her the confidence to pitch herself for a new job. She negotiated boldly, secured a significant salary hike, and landed the role within two months.

The result? Momentum. With every step, her belief became undeniable.

We have seen many women have challenging experiences shaping their crucibles.

Case Study: A leader who went through abuse by her uncle.

Below is one such real experience from Teena.

Teena was a confident and happy girl till she was six.

At the tender age of six, Teena's world shattered.

Her uncle abused her badly when no one was around.

She did not know how to process it or have the words to explain it, but she felt it daily.

A sense of hidden fear became her shadow as she grew up.

She stopped speaking up in class, even when she knew the correct answers. She withdrew, always staying in the background. Somewhere deep inside, she believed she was **small, powerless, unworthy**.

But she had a gift—an extraordinary mind for technology. Numbers, systems, logic—these did not hurt her. These made sense. They gave her control when nothing else did.

So, she built a career in tech.

She worked hard, delivering results that others took credit for. She had ideas that transformed systems, but she **hesitated** to voice them. She was **overlooked for promotions**, dismissed in meetings, and **underpaid** despite being the most intelligent person in the room.

Because fear still controlled her.

The same fear that told her at six to stay silent now told her to remain in her place at thirty-five.

For years, she accepted it. One day, she could not do it anymore.

She saw men—**less capable**, less hardworking—rise. She saw colleagues she had trained move ahead of her. She saw herself shrinking, disappearing, and she realized:

This was not her fault.

 Chapter 8: The Tactics: Win Without Fighting

But breaking free was not easy.

She tried reading self-help books. She took online courses. She even attempted to speak up in meetings. But the voice in her head—you are not powerful enough—never left.

She was unsure what to expect when she started practicing through the **Iron Lady Way**. It was another program, another promise.

At first, she resisted.

She stayed quiet when they asked her to talk about her biggest fear. When they pushed her to own her achievements, she shrugged them off. When they told her she was a leader, she laughed.

Slowly, she realized that her fears, which had been present since childhood, were **holding her back**! As part of the process, she followed the three-step process.

Step 1: Let go.

She let go of her fears and resentments, she declared. I let go of my fears and resentments, too.

She let go of the resentments slowly, and to maintain her calm, she built a sense of joy and energy within herself.

Step 2: Bring forth.

        Chapter 8: The Tactics: Win Without Fighting

She brought forth a sense of joy and happiness for herself and her children. She said I keep bringing this forth for my life and my children's happiness.

Step 3: Commit

She committed to her new dreams, accomplishments, and goals! She reaffirmed to herself that she will keep making this commitment a part of her life **EVERY DAY.**

For the first time, she believed she could be decisive.

It did not happen overnight.

Her voice trembled the first time she spoke up in a high-stakes meeting.

But she kept going.

And then, the shift happened.

Her strategies started getting noticed. Her confidence became undeniable.

She started **inspiring her team members to believe much more** in their goals and dreams, pushing them toward those much more.

The promotions followed. The leadership roles came. And soon, her income soared past a crore.

But the real victory was not just the money.

It was the moment she looked in the mirror and saw a woman who was no longer afraid.

Teena did not just break through the glass ceiling.

She shattered the chains that had held her since she was six.

Because once she let go of the fear, once she stepped into her power—nothing could stop her.

I have reached the crore-plus income benchmark using advanced winning tactics and dealing with my crucibles.

This is what is possible when you refuse to let your Crucibles define your future.

3. Maximize! Do not 'Balance'!

Women are often asked to **'Balance.'**

Unfortunately, under the guise of balance, they are asked to **'compromise.'**

Balance becomes the sugar-coated nonsense for **'compromise'!**

They are fed the illusion that they must be perfect and can "have it all" if they balance everything perfectly!

Chapter 8: The Tactics: Win Without Fighting

Men are often asked and measured by how high they have reached, while women are measured by how perfectly they've 'balanced' everything!

In the face of this, the tactics practice: **Maximize. Do not try and 'balance.'**

This is not another excuse to get women to **'do more'** or be perfect.

When you align, 'provide' double. When you 'mis-align,' clean up and communicate!

Keep the end in mind!

The principle of **'Maximize'** enables you to **'GET it DONE'** – instead of 'doing it.'

a. What Does It Mean to 'Maximize'?

Do less. Be more. Win big.

Maximization is not about grinding harder or stretching yourself thin—it is about cutting through the clutter and focusing on what moves the needle.

It is about strategy over struggle and impact over effort. It is knowing when to negotiate shamelessly, eliminate distractions, and make every action count.

Because real success is not about how much you do but how much impact you create. **That is how you win.**

   Chapter 8: The Tactics: Win Without Fighting

b. The Three Battlegrounds of Maximization

Winning is not about doing more—it is about getting the right things done!

i. Maximizing at Work

The higher you aim in your career, the better tactics you need to use. Here is how to make the most of your time and energy at work:

Start with the End Goal:

Before diving into any task, ask yourself—what is the actual outcome towards which I work? Focus on results, not just the amount of work you put in. Clarity beats effort every time.

Speak up from the beginning regarding What You Need:

From the start, speak up for the resources and support that will set you up for success. Clear communication and expectation-setting are game changers.

Stop Doing Everything Yourself:

It is tempting to take complete control but trying to do it all will only drain you. Not everything needs to be 100% perfect—sometimes, 80% is good enough. If perfection is necessary, step in at the critical stages rather than micromanaging the entire process.

     Chapter 8: The Tactics: Win Without Fighting

ii.   Personal Energy: Maximizing Energy & Focus

Research has repeatedly shown that leaders who manage their energy, not just their time, are far more successful.

For women to **'WIN'** in their lives, the first principle is to manage their energy. Not just their time.

The key is to focus. Eliminate distractions in many ways.

You have already lost if you are exhausted, distracted, or overwhelmed.

Focus on What Truly Matters

- **Eliminate the Unnecessary:**

Not everything on your to-do list is essential. Cut out tasks that do not serve your goal. The less time you spend on distractions, the more time you have for what moves the needle.

- **Work with Your Energy, Not Against It:**

Women's energy cycles differ from men's, but workplaces are not built with this in mind. Instead of pushing yourself to exhaustion, schedule your most important work during your peak energy hours. Stop forcing productivity—start aligning with your natural rhythm.

iii.   On the home front: Maximizing relationships and work

Leadership does not start and end at the office.

If you are compromising at home, it drains your ability to win at work.

- **Negotiate at Home as You Do at Work:**

Stop feeling guilty for getting help. Hiring a cook, a maid, or extra support does not make you less capable—it makes you smarter. The real power move? Freeing yourself up for what matters.

Negotiating and **hiring a maid** is as essential as finding the next significant role!

- **Talk It Out—Do not Assume:**

Just because something is important to you does not mean it is evident to everyone else. Have tough conversations. Set clear expectations. And when needed, say 'No'—with love, but firmly.

- **Start managing expectations with relationships:**

Wanting more—for your career, family, yourself—is not selfish. You do not have to prove your worth by running into the ground. You can have both—without breaking yourself in the process.

a. Case Study: A Woman's Place Is NOT in the Kitchen

Neha's story, in her own words:

'I grew up in a 'traditional joint family' where a woman's ambitions were always secondary to household responsibilities.

I struggled to balance everything with a whole house, two young school-going kids, and societal expectations pressing down on me. Yet, the most frustrating part was the responsibilities and the lack of understanding.

"Your husband earns well; why do you even need to work?"

"No one asked you to work, so don't expect support."

These words echoed around me, reinforcing the belief that my dreams were a burden, something extra that could be dismissed. On one side, I had my ambitions. On the other hand, I had endless obligations. And somewhere in between, I felt like I was losing myself.

When I joined the Iron Lady program, I was not looking for just another leadership lesson—I was searching for clarity, for a way to reclaim myself. And then, one line changed everything:

Leaders do not 'balance.' Leaders 'maximize'!

For years, I had been trying to balance. All it had brought me was exhaustion. I realized that alignment, not balance, was the key.

One exercise in the program opened my eyes. I had to list all the key relationships in my life—what I expected from them and what they expected from me. The results were startling.

Everyone was pulling in different directions, and I was caught in the middle, trying to please them all. No wonder I felt stuck.

That day, I decided. I was done with balance. It was time to maximize.

The first step was creating alignment, starting with the ones closest to me. I sat down with my daughter, my strongest ally.

She loved French and dreamed of studying there. I saw an opportunity.

"My hard work is to make this happen for you. If it's your dream, it's my dream too."

Her face lit up.

"Mom, we can do this?"

Just like that, I had my first supporter.

Next was my son. I explained our new mission—to help his sister achieve her dream.

He said without hesitation,

"I'm all IN, mom!"

With my children by my side, I turned to my husband. He had grown up with similar financial limitations, and sending our daughter abroad felt too big, too ambitious.

He asked,

          Chapter 8: The Tactics: Win Without Fighting

"What if we fail? Are we giving her a dream we cannot afford?"

I looked at him and said,

"As a team, we have never failed. If we do this together, we'll make it happen."

Our family had one goal. One direction.

Slowly, my in-laws and extended family saw the shift. People adjusted when I stopped justifying my choices and instead stood firm in them. The resistance weakened. Alignment replaced conflict.

Then, the pandemic hit. I had no maids, so I had to do more household work. My family still needed me, and my career was growing fast.

I had two choices—either break down or pitch again.

I started with the kids.

"Can you help?"

"We'll make tea and evening snacks, Mom!"

With them on board, I turned to my mother-in-law and husband.

"If we all share the load, we all win."

 Chapter 8: The Tactics: Win Without Fighting

At first, they hesitated. The change was uncomfortable. But I did not stop. I pitched multiple times, shamelessly demanding support. I refused to shrink my ambitions for the sake of maintaining peace.

Slowly, things started shifting. Small gestures—like someone opening the door when I was on a video call—became daily habits. Support came, not because I begged for it, but because I negotiated for it.

And then, something remarkable happened.

I got a **BIG promotion**.

My daughter scored the **highest marks of her life in her board exams**!

I was winning big.

My family was winning bigger!

My story is not about balance. It is about taking charge, demanding alignment, and leading without apology.'

4. The Unpredictable Game

Have you ever been cut off mid-sentence in a meeting?

Passed over for a promotion that should have been yours?

Hidden biases and glass ceilings could be treacherous. Toxic situations can drain your energy completely.

Here is the **five-step 'Unpredictable Game'** that has helped thousands of women overcome these challenges and take charge of their careers.

Step 1: Get Out of the 'Sitting Duck' Mode – Stop Waiting, Start Anticipating

Bias often works in ways we do not see—until it is too late. Instead of waiting to be overlooked, start noticing patterns and positioning yourself before making decisions.

What you can do:

- Create a **"power map"** of your workplace. Who influences promotions, projects, and visibility?

- Start building relationships before decisions are made.

Step 2: Be on the 'Attack' – Control the Narrative

Many women experience subtle (or not-so-subtle) biases, like being interrupted in meetings or dismissing their ideas.

The key is to bring awareness to these patterns and use facts, not frustration, to challenge them.

Your competitor or your challenger may have as much of a weakness – as much as you!

Find out what other people's weaknesses may be as much as you.

          Chapter 8: The Tactics: Win Without Fighting

What you can do:

- Keep a record of workplace patterns that limit your voice.

- Focus where you can be on the ATTACK and not just be defensive.

Step 3: Deliver Big Through Your Strengths and Showcase. Have a strategy based on your strengths!

Bias often downplays women's contributions. The best way to counter this is to make your work visible to benefit the organization.

What you can do:

- Make your wins part of the company's success story.

- In meetings, state your contributions confidently: "The new strategy I implemented reduced costs by 20 percent. Let us discuss how we can scale it."

Step 4: Be Unpredictable

Women are often boxed into stereotypes—too soft, too aggressive, too quiet, too emotional. The way out? Keep people guessing.

                    Chapter 8: The Tactics: Win Without Fighting

What you can do:

- Rotate between different leadership styles—be assertive when needed and collaborative when it serves the goal.

- Challenge perceptions by leading in ways people do not expect – suddenly changing your track.

Step 5: Win Without Fighting – Build Alliances, Not Enemies

Not everyone will immediately support you. Instead of wasting energy fighting the opposition, find a way to WIN so nobody wants to fight with you and concede your win.

What you can do:

- Showcase yourself so brilliantly that people do not want to 'fight' with you!

- Find ways to get enough people on your side – so that people feel it is not worth fighting against you.

Case Study: A CEO of a 100-Crore Company Who Was 'Stuck'

When Rajoshree joined the Iron Lady community, she was the CEO of a ₹100 crore company, carrying an ambition most would not dare voice aloud.

"In three years, I want to take my company to ₹1000 crores." She was not just another executive but a woman with a vision.

She immersed herself in the program, implementing every strategy, working late into the night, and writing down every step she needed to execute. But then, something broke. Just minutes into planning her company's future, she stopped writing. Her eyes welled up.

For ten minutes, she refused to speak. Finally, she whispered, "Rajesh, this is confidential." She was not someone who gossiped or played politics. But as the room reassured her, the truth unravelled.

"My nightmare began when I joined as the CEO two years ago. My boss, the company's Managing Director, was having an affair with the receptionist.

*He became insecure when I became the CEO. He changed the role of the receptionist and made her the **Head of Operations!**"*

Every decision Rajoshree needed to make was stuck!

Strategy? Stuck. Growth? Blocked. Her every move was undermined, yet she could not bring herself to call it out. She was trapped.

She sighed and said,

"I feel like a rubberstamp CEO. Helpless!"

She asked, **"Now tell me, what should I do?"**

The answer was in the tactics: First, stop **being a sitting duck!**

At first, she struggled.

As she followed the rituals in the program, one step at a time, she slowly built up the courage to do what no one expected.

She built her strengths and a clear roadmap using her strengths or the Shakti!

She kept focusing a lot more on what's possible.

She stopped sulking. She stopped complaining. She stopped fighting a battle that had no rules.

Instead, she became **unpredictable.**

One day, after weeks of preparation, she put on her biggest, brightest smile and walked into the office!

She organized an informal party with **friends and family members**!

She invited everyone, including the boss's wife!

　　　　Chapter 8: The Tactics: Win Without Fighting

"Madam, please come visit us in the office. We have a small get-together on Saturday. You are one of our guests."

No gossip. No backbiting. It's a perfectly executed move.

The wife, utterly unaware of what was happening behind the scenes, happily accepted the invitation. That Saturday, she walked into the office, mingling with employees, clueless about the ticking bomb that had just been placed in the MD's life.

While the rest of the office enjoyed snacks and drinks, only one person, the MD, was consumed by panic.

She did not have to say a word. **The message was loud and clear—never mess with Rajoshree.**

She no longer wasted her energy on the nonsense that others were throwing at her. She focused on what she did best: **building the company, growing the business, and proving her worth through impact and scale.**

Within months, she launched two brand-new services and stormed into the market. Sales exploded. Every week, she was closing deals worth **₹1-2 crores**. The company was growing at a speed no one had seen before.

By the middle of the year, something shifted. The same people who tried to push her out were whispering something new— **"Do not mess with Rajoshree. She is the winner."**

The board made it clear that **she was the head of the organization.** She no longer had to seek approval from anyone to make finance or strategy decisions.

     Chapter 8: The Tactics: Win Without Fighting

She did not have to destroy anyone to win, she did not have to stoop to their level, and she did not need politics.

She played to her strengths. She mastered the game. She **took control.**

Today, when people ask about her journey, the answer is simple: If you mess with her, you will not survive in the company. She is not here to take orders. She is here to lead.

5. Reflections

"The best leaders don't fight—they win without fighting!"

This chapter lays out some of the Tactics to WIN without fighting!

1. Draft your one-minute **"YES-Worthy"** statement today—including past wins and future vision. Practice it aloud, then pitch it to a mentor.

2. What are some of your beliefs that are holding you back? List down the steps you will take – to build unquestionable belief!

3. List down the areas where you want to WIN without fighting. Start exploring ways to WIN!

Remember: the woman who knows the tactics will win and grow. The one who does not know will not!

Which tactics will you use today to WIN Without Fighting?

                    Chapter 8: The Tactics: Win Without Fighting

Chapter 9: The C-Suite League

Women who understand and **master** the **'Business Warfare'** of **'Winning Without Fighting' tactics** find their way to the C-Suite—not by fighting harder but tactfully moving ahead.

They excel at **Winning** the **most brutal** wars for their organizations, their teams, and themselves **without fighting**!

Ready for the C-Suite!

1. C-Suite League: The 'Masters of Business Warfare'

"I am so proud of my progress! I have built a multimillion-dollar company. **I'm now supporting other women** to reach the C-Suite—and thrive there."

– Swapna Ponakampalli, President, C-Suite League

                                          Chapter 9: The C-Suite League

C-Suite League is a powerful community of senior women leaders who have **mastered** the **Art of Winning without Fighting**.

Here, members prepare to step into top executive roles by mastering four pillars of strengths.

Women in this League are on track – to become **CXOs / Managing Directors, Senior Vice Presidents, and CEOs** within the next few years, shaping industries and leading with authority.

For women ready to claim their place at the top—and stay there—these are the **four areas of mastery**.

Let's explore the four pillars.

Focus 1: Operational Excellence Mastery

The first step to reaching the C-suite is mastering the tactics to deliver big results consistently.

How do you manage complex teams and stakeholders, navigate challenging situations, engage in difficult conversations, and manage intense politics?

How can you accomplish these in the least time with the fewest resources?

Ready to rule the C-Suite!

The most **important mantra** to master these with ease is this:

If **you've managed a small team and project**, you **can** manage a **large team and project**.

Figure out how to extrapolate your skills and organize the resources and people; you can do it faster than most others!

To build Operational Excellence on your journey to the C-Suite, start by developing these core tactics:

- **Drive large teams (and manage senior leaders) confidently** – Learn to manage up, down, and across with authority. Define robust structures and understand and manage multiple layers of teams and stakeholders.

- **Master dealing with INTENSE corporate politics** – Being proactively at ease with intense politics (without getting *into* it) is a superpower. Decode people's agendas—remember, a rival's hostility often hides

                     Chapter 9: The C-Suite League

insecurity. Offer them a **"win"** that also aligns with your goals.

- **Delivering large-scale results**—High performance at this level means driving consistent impact at scale. Create and track leadership metrics (like stakeholder satisfaction or innovation ROI) and turn them into powerful narratives that showcase your impact and indispensability.

Sample C-Suite Ritual: "Stakeholder Chess"

Play the game before it begins. Every month, map out key stakeholders—their motivations, hidden agendas, and likely next moves.

Think two to three steps ahead. Anticipate their actions, align your strategy, and position yourself to win without confrontation.

Focus 2: Strategic 'Enemy-Centric' Planning / Business Strategy

Everyone's business is BUSINESS!

Speak the **BUSINESS language** and create **Business Strategies and Tactics**.

Just because you are part of a 'functional role,' if you stick to only the functional ideas, you will be considered a 'frog in the well.'

     Chapter 9: The C-Suite League

How can you master this fast?

Women who enter the corporate world end up with numerous 'enemies.

Some of them are obvious, and some of them are hidden.

Women who hesitate to differentiate or are worried about the 'competition' or enemies struggle to survive or reach the C-Suites.

The trick is not to **fight them head-on** but to **learn to Differentiate.**

So, how do you quickly break out and think like a business leader?

- **Create and drive strategies** – The enemy you 'choose' to fight with determines the height you reach. Identify and differentiate the 'right enemy.' Learn to share / and drive ideas using sharp business language by differentiating against the enemy chosen – so that you can drive strategic objectives, not just come across as a 'doer.'

- **Everyone's business is 'Business'** – people are hired to manage, drive, or scale the business. Understand the business perspectives and the levels for scaling or managing the business. Speak the **business language** wherever possible.

- **Focus on at least one BIG breakthrough idea every 3 months** – communicate the concept using 'business

 Chapter 9: The C-Suite League

language' that gets you 'noticed' so that you leverage it to remain focused on the big picture.

Sample C-Suite Ritual:

Craft 2–3 focused strategy presentations each month to sharpen your thinking and set the tone for what's ahead. Practice sharing them both formally and informally to build influence across all levels.

Focus 3: Mastery of 'Market,' Terrain, and Energy Centers

"If you can't understand and influence the **Energy Centers** in an organization, you are out of the game!"

Your ability to decode the market forces / terrain—where influence flows, where decisions crystallize, and where resistance festers—determines whether you rise to the top or not.

Understanding the big picture, the energy centers, and the overall 'market' is key.

Women in leadership must navigate strategically.

The Trick is to Stand Out—here's how

- **Decode the Terrain:** Identify **energy centers** (decision-makers, budget holders, cultural influencers). Spot **terrain hazards** (bureaucratic blocks, toxic alliances).

                    Chapter 9: The C-Suite League

Understand how to navigate your ideas / strategies and influence those.

- **Know and deal with Energy Centers: Fuel Allies**: Frame your initiatives as solutions to leaders' pain points. **Neutralize Hazards**: Reroute decisions through supportive stakeholders.

- **Understand the Market space intuitively:** Develop an intuitive ability to understand what's happening in the market space and the ecosystem – to make your communication and ideas relevant at the TOP.

Sample C-Suite Ritual:

Create 2–3 informal 'pitches' around your ideas or initiatives each month. Test them in casual conversations, gather feedback, refine your approach—and present them formally with impact when the moment is right.

Focus 4: Leadership and Functional Mastery

'Think upside down. Not just inside out!'

Leaders in C-Suites need to **influence** other senior–level individuals across various functions.

These leaders are distinguished by their ability to translate insights across functions, align diverse teams, and drive cross-functional collaboration.

Leaders in the C-Suites, hence, are needed to be the 'leaders of leaders!'

If you know only your function and can't speak confidently to people in other functions, you'll find it hard to connect with people – formally and informally.

Here's how you can develop this leadership edge:

- **Inspire others –**Understand the strengths, weaknesses, and blind spots of those around you. Learn practical tactics to support others in their career growth—and inspire them to aim higher and perform better.

- **Build a long-term roadmap for yourself and others –** Develop a clear, future-focused growth blueprint for yourself and your teams. Go beyond short-term wins and plan for lasting impact.

- **Understand other functions 'from the top' –**Gain a high-level perspective on how different functions operate from a leadership lens.

  For example, what does a CEO expect from the technology leadership team? Learn to think like a top leader across domains.

Sample C-Suite Ritual:

Study one function – from the eyes of a CEO, for a few minutes. Understand what the CEO expects from the function, what the KPIs are in that function, and what a leader at the C-Suite in that function is expected to do.

Case Study: Cancer to C-Suite and Crore Plus: The Strategic Comeback of Suman Mehta, SaaS Business Leader

How a Leader Transformed Adversity into 'Business Impact,' Secured a Crore-Plus Package, and Redefined C-Suite Influence!

The Shock: From Cancer Diagnosis

Suman Mehta was a high-performing product leader at a leading SaaS company in Bengaluru. Her career was on the rise when she was **diagnosed with cancer, a** life-altering moment that forced her to step back and focus on her health. She faced the treatment head-on, determined to return stronger.

But just as she began regaining her strength and looking forward to returning to work, another shock awaited her—termination. Her company informed her that her position was dissolved due to "business restructuring." She had survived cancer, only to find her career slipping away.

She realized this wasn't just about a lost job—it was about how she had positioned herself all along.

The Realization

Suman was always seen as having a strong product mind, delivering features, shipping products, and managing execution. But she had never positioned herself as a business-critical leader who drove growth, revenue, and competitive strategy.

At an Iron Lady session, one insight hit her hard:

> "Your product expertise is valuable, but companies don't pay for features—they pay for business impact. Sell that."

She realized she needed to shift her narrative—not as a product specialist but as a strategic business driver.

The Turning Point: Thinking Beyond Execution

That one sentence reframed her entire approach. Suman recognized that product leadership alone wasn't enough—she had to speak the language of business and show how her work directly impacted revenue, growth, and market expansion.

This shift in thinking became the foundation of her comeback.

Tactic 1: The Business-Centric Pitch – Shifting from Product to Profit

Suman began aligning her pitch with business outcomes—not product outputs.

The **"Revenue-Driven Pitch"** Approach:

- **Identify Business Pain Points**
  She analyzed customer churn and realized mid-market clients were dropping off due to poor onboarding. The data showed a 15% higher churn rate than competitors.

    Chapter 9: The C-Suite League

- **Pitch Example**
  "By redesigning onboarding, we can cut churn by 30% and add ₹20 crore in ARR. Let me lead this initiative."

- **Aligning with Executive Priorities**
  She tied her solution to top-level metrics: customer retention, expansion revenue, and profitability.

- **Skip Middle Management, Pitch to Decision-Makers**
  Instead of waiting for her manager's approval, Suman pitched directly to the CPO, positioning it as an urgent strategic need.

Result:

She was given 90 days to execute her plan—bypassing usual bottlenecks. The impact? A **25% drop in churn and a 40% increase i**n upsell revenue.

Tactic 2: Building a Differentiated C-Suite Brand

Suman knew delivering impact wasn't enough; she had to be *seen* as a strategic leader.

She started building a brand beyond product leadership, showcasing her as a business transformation expert.

Strategic Positioning Playbook:

- **Industry Influence:**
  She began publishing thought leadership content focused on SaaS monetization and revenue strategy, catching the attention of investors, peers, and

 Chapter 9: The C-Suite League

analysts.

- **Internal Credibility:**
  She hosted exclusive roundtables with senior leadership to discuss revenue growth strategies, elevating her influence within the company.

- **Speaking Engagements:**
  She began speaking at industry panels, shifting how people perceived her—from a functional expert to a forward-thinking business leader.

Result:
Competing startups and consulting firms started approaching her with crore-plus offers. Her own company took notice and re-evaluated her strategic value.

Tactic 3: The Crore-Club Negotiation – Leveraging Business Wins for Maximum Growth

Armed with solid results and external offers, Suman was ready to renegotiate her salary, role, influence, and autonomy.

Her impact-backed pitch:

> "You've seen the numbers. **I don't just build products—I scale revenue.** If this company wants to dominate the market, I need the resources to make that happen."

Outcome:

- Salary: ₹1.1 crore—double her pre-illness package

 Chapter 9: The C-Suite League

- Title: Promoted to VP of Growth & Strategy
- Autonomy: Granted full ownership of an Innovation Lab to lead high-impact initiatives

She didn't ask for more. She *proved* why she deserved it.

Her defining quote:

"I stopped thinking like a product manager and started thinking like a boardroom leader. That changed everything."

Key Takeaways from Suman's Playbook

- **Frame Your Work as Business Impact:**
  Talk about growth, profitability, and market leadership—not just features or execution.

- **Own Your Narrative:**
  Build a C-suite identity that sets you apart inside your organization and the industry.

- **Negotiate Relentlessly:**
  Use real business wins and external validation to command better pay, more prominent roles, and strategic authority.

Chapter 9: The C-Suite League

2. Reflections:

How can you master the art of '**Winning Without Fighting**' in business warfare to advance to the C-Suite strategically?

Reflect on your work today:

Are you seen as a hard worker or a top business leader?

What actions can you take today – to recreate your brand as a top business leader?

Step back, recalibrate, and show where decisions are made, not just where tasks are assigned!

Are you willing to be the '**Shameless Lady**' ruling the **C-Suite**?

Chapter 9: The C-Suite League

Chapter 10: On a mission: The Iron Lady Army!

*"I have accomplished **twenty-three 'Big Hairy Audacious Goals (BHAGs)' over the last 3 years!"***

> \- Lakshmi Nayak, President, Bengaluru chapter, Iron Lady Army

Thousands of women have reached top positions using the **Iron Lady Way** at companies like **Amazon, Google, Microsoft, Walmart, TCS, Infosys, Big 4s,** and hundreds of others.

They have united as **commanders** to build the Iron Lady Army selflessly, inspiring others to win.

"I've also made it **my purpose–** to inspire a **million women to reach the top**, after reaching the top myself, using these tactics over the years."

> \- Neha Agarwal, GSI India Leader at Amazon Web Services (AWS).

1. An Army: Not just a community

"For us at the **Iron Lady Army**, a **million women at the top** is not just a slogan. It is a **war cry**! We push each other every day to WIN!"

> \- Rownmani C, President, Iron Lady Army

'Wars' that women need to win to move ahead need an 'Army' like mindset!

Most communities (even those focused on women) do not work well in **enabling them to win**—they get diluted, and the focus shifts away!

Iron Lady Army takes a pledge!

When we began the journey, we requested women to unite, volunteer with us, and build the **Iron Lady Army**!

Below, we share how the **Commanders of this Army** have created a movement to **transform and inspire** generations of women.

This is an Army where women come together – to **learn** from each other, **support** each other, and **celebrate wins** together!

Every army member focuses on the mission: **A million women at the TOP.**

 Chapter 10: On a mission: The Iron Lady Army!

The Commanders ask:

'Can we **celebrate** women reaching Big Goals every day
instead of judging others!'

Can we privately support women in addressing
vulnerabilities and weaknesses and find **real-world solutions**
to move ahead?'

a. Intense Practice – focus on 'Capabilities.'

Traditional learning often focuses on acquiring knowledge.

However, we must enable people to undergo intense practice
sessions when focusing on 'Capability' development.

The focus is on 'Mastery' of capabilities – rather than just
'understanding.'

We have experienced that women can absorb and develop
much more when there is a clear focus and intensity on the
capabilities that matter.

Through various simulations and role-plays, almost real-time
feedback, and Live challenges, women rapidly develop
breakthrough capabilities.

b. Private, small group huddles

 "My husband feels **insecure about how I'm growing so fast**."

For many women in leadership, the most brutal battles are not just in the boardroom—they are the silent struggles no one talks about.

Workplace politics, bias, and unspoken expectations make it hard to voice challenges openly.

Through confidential, private small group mentoring sessions, women discuss the most challenging situations, understand each other's challenges, and seek support from mentors to overcome them.

The dedicated group of **program leaders**, who come together with the **passion to contribute tirelessly**, creates an **exceptional impact** on every Iron Lady!

c. Enabling Each Other to WIN

"So, what's your next Big Hairy Audacious Goal." asked a mentor at Iron Lady!

Given that the focus is always on Winning, we solve challenges with women's next goals in mind.

When people solve challenges in this context, they handle challenges much better.

We have learned that when women come together to support each other in Winning, they create miracles together.

　　　　Chapter 10: On a mission: The Iron Lady Army!

This focus enables Meaningful networking – with deeper connections – purposeful networking instead of just hanging around together.

2. Diverse backgrounds and voices

In the Iron Lady Army, women come from diverse backgrounds.

Below are some of the diverse backgrounds and how role models and 'commanders' find a way of inspiring them!

The CEOs

Many of the women who have gone on to become top CEOs inspire other women to reach CEO positions.

"I was able to deal with the most demanding challenges of my personal and professional life, thanks to the Army.

Here is my message for women who are not even dreaming of becoming CEOs. You have it in you. Go for it!" says Shobha Patil, CEO of Sankey Solutions

Entrepreneurs and Businesswomen

'A man's business is a 'real business.' A woman's business is a hobby!'

Women entrepreneurs who have taken their companies to the top come together to destroy the above perception and inspire other women to be successful.

"Becoming a top entrepreneur was just the beginning for me. True fulfilment came from inspiring and supporting thousands of women to rise alongside me.**"**

- Pushpalatha MS, CEO, Prameya, Cofounder, Garbhagudi

Women in Technology

'Women in technology don't understand the **big picture**!'

Women in technology who have gone through the most demanding challenges, like the misconception above, and reached C-Suite positions in technology support others in doing the same.

"We can create a new world with our technology strategies!"
- Ranisuneela Motru, Engineering Leader at Google.

"Women in Technology should speak the language that the people at the top understand. Technology that creates global scale and that turns around businesses!"
- Sirisha Arza, Director, Product Delivery

"As Technology leaders, we need to speak the language of Technology for scale and bring about a transformational difference daily!"
- Padmashree Suresh, Senior Leader at HCLTech.

Women in Human Resources

Women in human resources are often considered 'rangoli makers' and support people!

Top HR leaders who have dealt with these bias challenges and reached top HR positions inspire others to reach new heights.

"Women in Human Resources need to think more about how they can drive the business forward, not just about HR,"
- Nithya Chandar, President of Iron Lady Delhi Army.

Women in Sales

'Women are unfit for the **gruelling** sales leadership roles.'

Women who have broken these biases and barriers have reached the top. They are now showcasing to others how it's done!

I have experienced firsthand the kind of challenges that women face and how they can overcome any challenge. Hence, I take pleasure in seeing other women in Sales and tough profiles WIN,"

- Poornima Dikshit, Enterprise Sales Leader

     Chapter 10: On a mission: The Iron Lady Army!

Women in Delivery and operations

Leaders who have reached top delivery positions train them on how it is done.

"Do not get lost in just the day-to-day. Keep your head in the stars. Embrace Technology for scale as well!"

> \- Padmashree Yandagoudar, President, Iron Lady Army, Pune

Women in finance or Admin

They find it challenging to build a brand for themselves – since they do not speak the language beyond finance or administration.

"If you can manage the entire finances of a company – you can manage many things easily!"
> \- Bindu Bhat, Partner at Guardian Capital

Doctors, scientists, and other specialists

Women in specialized fields find it challenging to understand and deal with challenges outside their domain expertise to reach the next level.

Chapter 10: On a mission: The Iron Lady Army!

"I've started thinking like a doctorpreneur, using these tactics, and grown quite a bit. I've realized that those who think on these lines grow much more."
- Dr. Asha S Vijay, Founder and Medical Director, Garbhagudi

100 Board Members: the 'decision-makers'

Most places do not support the development of capabilities or roadmaps for women to reach decision-making or 'board positions.'

Owing to this, women struggle to understand the meaning and significance of **various 'boards',** such as functional leadership boards.

The 100 Board Members Community is a unique community of Women who have developed **Breakthrough Capabilities** using the unique **Shakti** methodology.

These women are ready to roar at the **decision-making 'board positions!'**

"I have found immense pleasure in mentoring others to reach and sustain senior-level positions, including decision-making operational board-level positions. The impact that we are making is tremendous!"

- Moona Ssahni, Founder & CEO of Monaargy Consultancy, President, '100 Board Members' Community.

 Chapter 10: On a mission: The Iron Lady Army!

3. Focus on 'breakthroughs' that matter!

As women develop winning tactics, they need to deal with the most demanding challenges that matter quickly.

The Army enables women to focus on **breakthroughs that matter** and to deal with the toughest challenges.

The following are the three most critical challenges that we have solved together.

a. Getting New Jobs and new roles

"How many children do you have?" the interviewer asked her.

We have seen many brilliant women who are excellent in their jobs and have decades of experience but are not confident in attending interviews or do not know how to prepare. They often fail badly.

Women experience biases / challenges and find it difficult to differentiate or stand out in those interviews.

Most **'job platforms'** are built with men in mind. They do not support women in dealing with the questions and challenges that women face.

When their resumes come across as replicas of others, they find it hard to differentiate themselves or speak powerfully about themselves.

In the Iron Lady Army, women build powerful resumes using templates that have worked brilliantly for other women.

They create their '**Differentiated Leadership Brand,**' which helps them communicate their strengths and leadership presence through powerful stories.

Women learn to stand out during Interviews through the mocks with 'buddies.

We have experienced that women who are better prepared through these mocks get way more opportunities than others.

b. Fast-Tracking Growth at Work

"My boss got upset once when I shared an idea in a meeting. After that, I stopped speaking up in meetings. **I could not find the courage again."** Suguna mentioned it on her first day at Iron Lady.

The challenges women face in the workplace keep changing based on the situation.

Women who prepare better for those challenges grow much faster than those who do not.

　　　　Chapter 10: On a mission: The Iron Lady Army!

Below are some of the challenges women prepare for –
proactively in the Army.

- **Managing 'Bosses':**
  Preparing yourself for managing distinct types of bosses
  and super-bosses takes you ahead.

- **Managing teams confidently:**
  Women experience that some of their team members do
  not like 'woman boss'! Preparing to deal with the most
  formidable team members and creating a winning team
  are critical aspects of success as a leader.

- **Dealing with Politics or Bias:**
  Navigating a maze of politics, hidden biases, and subtle
  comments while trying to stay authentic is a critical and
  constant challenge that women need to master.

- **Preparing for the Toughest projects:**
  Leaders must make a difference from Day 1 in a new role
  or project. Women who fail to do this often catch up in
  their careers, which can limit growth.

- **Preparing for appraisal discussions!**
  Women who 'prepare' for the promotion discussion – do
  better than those who do not. Army members excel at
  these by using the pitches and tactics to win.

c. Starting and Scaling Businesses

When I approached investors for funding, they asked, **"Do you
have anyone else as a co-founder?"** I intuitively knew they

 Chapter 10: On a mission: The Iron Lady Army!

were hinting at a **male partner**. Rashmi shared this experience.

Women founders do not just build businesses—they break the most significant barriers. From securing clients to scaling operations, every step comes with challenges that men often do not face.

Pitching to clients, building a strong business model, managing a team, and navigating the complexities of scaling are not just skills; they are survival tools for women entrepreneurs.

Too many brilliant women founders or business owners struggle **alone**, unsure where to turn for guidance.

Finding the **right mentors**, making bold decisions, and leading with confidence are areas where women demonstrate power and confidence in this community!

4. Region-Specific Challenges and Chapters

"The challenges women face in Mumbai are vastly different from those in Bengaluru. But our commitment to reaching the top is the same."

- Ankita Mehta, President, Iron Lady Mumbai Army.

Women from different regions face different leadership barriers and different opportunities.

Various chapters of Iron Lady – and the leaders from those chapters – are paving the way for their communities to grow.

Following are some observations about the regions:

- In some regions, **family pressures** are much higher on women than in other regions.
- Opportunities for women in various regions vary based on the industries / market situations in those regions.
- Based on the backgrounds and the cultures of various regions, women from various regions develop diverse types of natural strengths

Below are some of the examples of the regional variations:

a. Bengaluru: The Technology and Start-up Hub

Twenty-seven of the first one hundred women who reached the **crore plus income** are from the Bengaluru **chapter**.

Compared to many other regions, Bengaluru has the highest number of women in technology, AI, Machine Learning, and start-ups who have reached crore-plus incomes.

Women in Bengaluru bring the spirit of innovation and scale to businesses that they are a part of.

b. Mumbai: The Business capital of India

Twenty-four women from Mumbai have reached the crore plus yearly incomes out of the **first one hundred** in the Iron Lady Community.

                    Chapter 10: On a mission: The Iron Lady Army!

The city's high-energy culture often provides opportunities for women in business, banking, and finance roles to grow much faster than others.

Women in Mumbai bring the utmost professionalism, incredible capabilities, and drive to grow in their careers.

c. Delhi: Consulting, Technology, and education hub

Women in the Iron Lady Community in Semiconductors, technology, and education are growing much faster than other Delhi industries.

We find the most powerful and assertive women who hunger to win at any cost in Delhi.

Eighteen women from Delhi have reached the **crore plus income** out of the first one hundred in the Iron Lady Community.

d. Other regions / cities

Hyderabad and **Pune** regions are upcoming regions where women leaders continue to drive innovation and leadership.

These cities have seen tremendous growth in women leading and driving exceptional results over the last few years.

We have eight women, each from Hyderabad and Pune – who have reached crore-plus incomes.

We also have Chennai with three women who have reached the crore plus income.

                     Chapter 10: On a mission: The Iron Lady Army!

Cities like Kolkata and many other tier-2 / tier-3 cities are to watch out for – with many outstanding leaders from those cities coming up amazingly fast.

5. The Future

"We are, together, creating a world where dreaming and going after our **dreams is NOT considered Shameless** anymore for women."

- Sujata Patnaik, President, Iron Lady Army, Hyderabad.

"We come together in Chennai to create the miracles that we earlier thought were impossible for women in Chennai!"

- Vimalaasree Anandhan, President, Iron Lady Army, Chennai

"Women in the East and North-east are committed to creating a new world for the women here!"

- Jayeeta Choudhury, President, Iron Lady Army, Kolkatta

"We are not just here to **compete**. We are here to **win together** and enable others to **win**!

     Chapter 10: On a mission: The Iron Lady Army!

6. Reflections

In a world where women are often told to 'balance', the Iron Lady Army is built on a different belief—that women can WIN and pull other women up.

Do reflect upon:

How can you create support systems that enable you to keep moving forward?

Success is not a solo journey—it is built on the strength of those beside us.

Together, can we create a **world** through the **power** of **Empathy**?

A new beginning

As we conclude '**The Shameless Lady**,' we face these questions:

- What additional steps can we take to create a significantly larger, global movement that inspires **generations** and **millions** of women?

- How can we create **thousands** of more **role models** across the globe?

- How can we inspire more women (and men) and more powerful **partners** to join forces with us to drive the movement forward?

- How can we let **every woman** know:

You are NOT alone!

You have **THE Shakti** within you.

Your struggles can be overcome.

Your dreams are important and can be accomplished!

You CAN reach the TOP!

The stories in **'The Shameless Lady'** testify to what's possible when women are empowered and supported through a powerful platform.

We have tried our best to share insights and tactics in this book to help women in your journey.

Through our experiences at Head Held High and Iron Lady, we aim to inspire generations of women to achieve greater success.

Do reach out if you can benefit from this movement or contribute to this purpose.

If you're keen to be part of this mission, please reach out to us at admin@iamironlady.com or visit iamironlady.com

Thank you for joining us on this journey.

We look forward to seeing you, with us, on the journey towards:

A million women at the TOP!

Acknowledgements

We are deeply grateful to the incredible people who have shaped **Iron Lady**'s journey and the book.

Our co-founders at Iron Lady, **Simon Newman, Sridhar Sambandam**, and **Chitra Talwar** – your insights, lessons, and unwavering support have been instrumental in shaping the ideas in these pages.

Our **parents** – you gave us the courage to **dream beyond the boundaries** of our **small village**. We owe everything to you.

Our **daughters** – you **inspire us** daily to dream for a better world.

Our **family and friends** – you have stood by us through every challenge and triumph.

Our team at **Iron Lady** – you created the magic with us.

Our **investors** at Iron Lady – your trust and commitment have fueled this mission.

Our co-founders at Head Held High, **Sunil Savara, and Madan Padaki** – your continuous support has been a foundation of strength for life.

Our inspirational mentors and supporters, such as **Anand Sudarshan** and **Arsh Maini**, and many more – your generosity has enabled us.

The **Program Leaders, mentors**, and **volunteers** at **Iron Lady** – you created the platform and the movement; you are the backbone of this movement.

To **every Iron Lady**, your unwavering dedication and belief in our purpose have turned it into a reality.

Together, let's continue to create a world where every woman WINs.

Thank you!